PRAISE FOR *DEBATING AMERICAN HISTORY*

"Debating American History repositions the discipline of history as one that is rooted in discovery, investigation, and interpretation."
—Ingrid Dineen-Wimberly,
University of California, Santa Barbara

"Debating American History is an excellent replacement for a 'big assignment' in a course. Offering a way to add discussion to a class, it is also a perfect 'active learning' assignment, in a convenient package."
—Gene Rhea Tucker, Temple College

"The advantage that *Debating American History* has over other projects and texts currently available is that it brings a very clear and focused organization to the notion of classroom debate. The terms of each debate are clear. The books introduce students to historiography and primary sources. Most of all, the project re-envisions the way that US history should be taught. No other textbook or set of teaching materials does what these books do when taken together as the sum of their parts."
—Ian Hartman, University of Alaska

DEBATING AMERICAN HISTORY

THE POWHATANS AND THE ENGLISH
IN THE SEVENTEENTH-CENTURY CHESAPEAKE

DEBATING AMERICAN HISTORY

Series Editors: Joel M. Sipress, David J. Voelker

DEBATING AMERICAN HISTORY

THE POWHATANS AND THE ENGLISH IN THE SEVENTEENTH-CENTURY CHESAPEAKE

David J. Voelker

UNIVERSITY OF WISCONSIN—GREEN BAY

NEW YORK   OXFORD
OXFORD UNIVERSITY PRESS

Oxford University Press is a department of the University of Oxford.
It furthers the University's objective of excellence in research, scholarship,
and education by publishing worldwide. Oxford is a registered trade mark of
Oxford University Press in the UK and certain other countries.

Published in the United States of America by Oxford University Press
198 Madison Avenue, New York, NY 10016, United States of America.

For titles covered by Section 112 of the US Higher Education
Opportunity Act, please visit www.oup.com/us/he for the latest
information about pricing and alternate formats.

Library of Congress Cataloging-in-Publication Data
Names: Voelker, David Joseph, author.
Title: The Powhatans and the English in the 17th-century Chesapeake / David
  J. Voelker, University of Wisconsin-Green Bay.
Description: First edition. | New York : Oxford University Press, [2020] |
  Series: Debating American history | Includes index.
Identifiers: LCCN 2018058944| ISBN 9780190057053 (pbk.) | ISBN 9780190057183
  (ebook)
Subjects: LCSH: Powhatan Indians—Chesapeake Bay Region (Md. and
  Va.)— History—17th century. | Powhatan Indians—Chesapeake Bay Region
  (Md. and Va.)—History—Sources. | Chesapeake Bay Region (Md. and
  Va.)—History—17th century—Sources.
Classification: LCC E99.P85 V64 2019 | DDC 975.5004/97347—dc23 LC record available
at https://lccn.loc.gov/2018058944

Printing number: 9 8 7 6 5 4 3 2 1
Printed by LSC Communications, Inc., United States of America

To my many teachers—past and present, younger and older—who inspire me to keep asking questions.

TABLE OF CONTENTS

LIST OF MAPS AND FIGURES

Maps

Figures

ABOUT THE AUTHOR

David J. Voelker holds a PhD in United States history from the University of North Carolina at Chapel Hill. He is Associate Professor of Humanities and History at the University of Wisconsin–Green Bay, where he teaches early American and environmental history. He served as the co-director of the Wisconsin Teaching Fellows & Scholars program from 2013 to 2019. He has published numerous articles and book chapters on American cultural, religious, and political history. He has also written essays on teaching and learning history, including "The End of the History Survey Course: The Rise and Fall of the Coverage Model," coauthored with Joel M. Sipress, *Journal of American History* 97 (March 2011): 1050–1066, which won the 2012 Maryellen Weimer Scholarly Work on Teaching and Learning Award. He co-edited *Big Picture Pedagogy: Finding Interdisciplinary Solutions to Common Learning Problems* (Jossey Bass, 2017) with Regan A. R. Gurung. He serves as co-editor of *Debating American History* with Joel M. Sipress.

ACKNOWLEDGMENTS

We owe gratitude to Aeron Haynie, Regan Gurung, and Nancy Chick for introducing us and pairing us to work on the Signature Pedagogies project many years ago, as well as to the UW System's Office of Professional and Instructional Development (OPID), which supported that endeavor. Brian Wheel, formerly with Oxford University Press, helped us develop the idea for *Debating American History* and started the project rolling. We want to thank Charles Cavaliere at Oxford for taking on the project and seeing it through to publication, and Anna Russell for her excellent production work. Joel thanks the University of Wisconsin–Superior for support from a sabbatical, and David thanks the University of Wisconsin–Green Bay for support from a Research Scholar grant. David would also like to thank his colleagues in humanities, history, and First Nations Studies, who have been supportive of this project for many years, and Joel thanks his colleagues in the Department of Social Inquiry. Thanks also to the reviewers of this book: Ian Hartman, University of Alaska Anchorage; Melanie Benson Taylor, Dartmouth College; Todd Romero, University of Houston; Philip Levy, University of South Florida; Ingrid Dineen-Wimberly , U of Calif., Santa Barbara and U of La Verne; Kristin Hargrove, Grossmont College; Melanie Beals Goan, University of Kentucky; Paul Hart, Texas State University; Ross A. Kennedy, Illinois State University; Scott Laderman, University of Minnesota, Duluth; John Putnam, San Diego State University; Matt Tribbe, University of Houston; Linda Tomlinson, Fayetteville State University; Shauna Hann, United States Military Academy; Michael Holm, Boston University; Raymond J. Krohn, Boise State University; Joseph Locke, University of Houston-Victoria; Ted Moore, Salt Lake Community College; Andrew L. Slap, East Tennessee State University; Matthew J. Clavin, University of Houston; Amani Marshall, Georgia State University; Luke Harlow, University of Tennessee, Knoxville; Matthew Pinsker, Dickinson College; Tyina Steptoe, University of Arizona; Daniel Vivian, University of Louisville; Robert J. Allison, Suffolk University, Boston; and Joshua Fulton, Moraine Valley Community College. We are also indebted to our colleagues (too numerous to mention) who have advanced the Scholarship of Teaching and Learning within the field of history. Without their efforts, this project would not have been possible.

SERIES INTRODUCTION

Although history instruction has grown richer and more varied over the past few decades, many college-level history teachers remain wedded to the coverage model, whose overriding design principle is to cover huge swaths of history, largely through the use of textbooks and lectures. The implied rationale supporting the coverage model is that students must be exposed to a wide array of facts, narratives, and concepts to have the necessary background both to be effective citizens and to study history at a more advanced level—something that few students actually undertake. Although coverage-based courses often afford the opportunity for students to encounter primary sources, the imperative to cover an expansive body of material dominates these courses; and the main assessment technique, whether implemented through objective or written exams, is to require students to identify or reproduce authorized knowledge.

Unfortunately, the coverage model has been falling short of its own goals since its very inception in the late nineteenth century. Educators and policymakers have been lamenting the historical ignorance of American youth going back to at least 1917, as Stanford professor of education Sam Wineburg documented in his illuminating exposé of the history of standardized tests of historical knowledge.[1] In 2010, the *New York Times* declared that "History is American students' worst subject," basing this judgment on yet another round of abysmal standardized test scores.[2] As we have documented in our own historical research, college professors over the past century have episodically criticized the coverage model and offered alternatives. Recently, however, college-level history instructors have been forming a scholarly community to improve the teaching of the introductory course by doing research that includes rigorous analysis of student learning. A number of historians who have

---

1 Sam Wineburg, "Crazy for History," *Journal of American History* 90 (March 2004): 1401–1414.
2 Sam Dillon, "U.S. Students Remain Poor at History, Tests Show," *New York Times*, June 14, 2011. Accessed online at http://www.nytimes.com/2011/06/15/education/15history.html?emc=eta1&pagewanted=print.

become involved in this discipline-based pedagogical research, known as the Scholarship of Teaching and Learning (SoTL), have begun to mount a challenge to the coverage model.[3]

Not only has the coverage model often achieved disappointing results by its own standards, it also proves ineffective at helping students learn how to think historically, which has long been a stated goal of history education. As Lendol Calder argued in a seminal 2006 article, the coverage model works to "cover up" or "conceal" the nature of historical thinking.[4] The eloquent lecture or the unified textbook narrative reinforces the idea that historical knowledge consists of a relatively straightforward description of the past. Typical methods of covering content hide from students not only the process of historical research—the discovery and interpretation of sources—but also the ongoing and evolving discussions among historians about historical meaning. In short, the coverage model impedes historical thinking by obscuring the fact that history is a complex, interpretative, and argumentative discourse.

Informed by the scholarship of the processes of teaching and learning, contemporary reformers have taken direct aim at the assumption that factual and conceptual knowledge must precede more sophisticated forms of historical study. Instead, reformers stress that students must learn to think historically by doing—at a novice level—what expert historians do.[5]

With these ideas in mind, we thus propose an argument-based model for teaching the introductory history course. In the argument-based model, students participate in a contested, evidence-based discourse about the human past. In other words, students are asked to argue about history. And by arguing, students develop the dispositions and habits of mind that are central to the discipline of history.[6] As the former American Historical Association (AHA) president Kenneth Pomeranz noted in late 2013, historians should consider seeing general education history courses as valuable "not for the sake of 'general

---

3   See Lendol Calder, "Uncoverage: Toward a Signature Pedagogy for the History Survey," *Journal of American History* 92 (March 2006): 1358–1370; Joel M. Sipress and David J. Voelker, "The End of the History Survey Course: The Rise and Fall of the Coverage Model," *Journal of American History* 97 (March 2011): 1050–1066; and Penne Restad, "American History Learned, Argued, and Agreed Upon," in Michael Sweet and Larry K. Michaelson, eds., *Team-Based Learning in the Social Sciences and Humanities*, 159–180 (Sterling, VA: Stylus, 2012). For an overview of the Scholarship of Teaching and Learning (SoTL) in history, see Joel M. Sipress and David Voelker, "From Learning History to Doing History: Beyond the Coverage Model," in *Exploring Signature Pedagogies: Approaches to Teaching Disciplinary Habits of Mind*, pp. 19–35, edited by Regan Gurung, Nancy Chick, and Aeron Haynie (Stylus Publishing, 2008). Note also that the International Society for the Scholarship of Teaching and Learning in History was formed in 2006. See http://www.indiana.edu/~histsotl/blog/.

4   Calder, "Uncoverage," 1362–1363.

5   For influential critiques of the "facts first" assumption, see Sam Wineburg, "Crazy for History," *Journal of American History* 90 (March 2004), 1401–1414; and Calder, "Uncoverage."

6   For discussions of argument-based courses, see Barbara E. Walvoord and John R. Breihan, "Arguing and Debating: Breihan's History Course," in Barbara E. Walvoord and Lucille P. McCarthy, *Thinking and Writing in College: A Naturalistic Study of Students in Four Disciplines* (Urbana, IL: National Council of Teachers of English, 1990), 97–143; Todd Estes, "Constructing the Syllabus: Devising a Framework for Helping Students Learn to Think Like Historians," *History Teacher* 40 (February 2007), 183–201; Joel M. Sipress, "Why Students Don't Get Evidence and What We Can Do About It," *The History Teacher* 37 (May 2004), 351–363; and David J. Voelker, "Assessing Student Understanding in Introductory Courses: A Sample Strategy," *The History Teacher* 41 (August 2008): 505–518.

knowledge' but for the intellectual operations you can teach."[7] Likewise, the AHA "Tuning Project" defines the discipline in a way much more consistent with an argument-based course than with the coverage model:

> History is a set of evolving rules and tools that allows us to interpret the past with clarity, rigor, and an appreciation for interpretative debate. It requires evidence, sophisticated use of information, and a deliberative stance to explain change and continuity over time. As a profoundly public pursuit, history is essential to active and empathetic citizenship and requires effective communication to make the past accessible to multiple audiences. As a discipline, history entails a set of professional ethics and standards that demand peer review, citation, and toleration for the provisional nature of knowledge.[8]

We have designed *Debating American History* with these values in mind.

In the coverage-based model, historical knowledge is seen as an end in itself. In the argument-based model, by contrast, the historical knowledge that students must master serves as a body of evidence to be employed in argument and debate. While the ultimate goal of the coverage approach is the development of a kind of cultural literacy, the argument-based history course seeks to develop historical modes of thinking and to encourage students to incorporate these modes of thinking into their daily lives. Particularly when housed within a broader curriculum that emphasizes engaged learning, an argument-based course prepares students to ask useful questions in the face of practical problems and challenges—whether personal, professional, or civic. On encountering a historical claim, such as those that frequently arise in political discussions, they will know how to ask important questions about context, evidence, and logic. In this way, the argument-based course fulfills the discipline's longstanding commitment to the cultivation of engaged and informed citizens.[9]

While there is no single correct way to structure an argument-based course, such courses do share a number of defining characteristics that drive course design.[10] In particular, argument-based courses include these elements:

1. THEY ARE ORGANIZED AROUND SIGNIFICANT HISTORICAL QUESTIONS ABOUT WHICH HISTORIANS THEMSELVES DISAGREE.

Argument-based courses are, first and foremost, question-driven courses in which "big" historical questions (rather than simply topics or themes) provide the overall organizational

---

7   Kenneth Pomeranz, "Advanced History for Beginners: Why We Should Bring What's Best about the Discipline into the Gen Ed Classroom," *Perspectives on History* (November 2013), at http://www.historians.org/publications-and-directories/perspectives-on-history/november-2013/advanced-history-for-beginners-why-we-should-bring-whats-best-about-the-discipline-into-the-gen-ed-classroom.

8   This definition reflects the state of the Tuning Project as of September 2013. For more information, see "AHA History Tuning Project: 2013 History Discipline Core," at https://www.historians.org/teaching-and-learning/tuning-the-history-discipline/2013-history-discipline-core. Accessed January 31, 2019.

9   As recently as 2006, the AHA's Teaching Division reasserted the importance of history study and scholarship in the development of globally aware citizens. Patrick Manning, "Presenting History to Policy Makers: Three Position Papers," *Perspectives: The Newsmagazine of the American Historical Association* 44 (March 2006), 22–24.

10   Our approach to course design is deeply influenced by Grant Wiggins and Jay McTighe, *Understanding by Design*, 2nd ed. (Upper Saddle River, NJ: Pearson Education, 2006).

structure. A "big" historical question is one about which historians themselves disagree and that has broad academic, intellectual, or cultural implications. Within these very broad parameters, the types of questions around which a course may be organized can vary greatly. The number of "big" questions addressed, however, must be relatively limited in number (perhaps three to five over the course of a typical fifteen-week semester), so that students can pursue the questions in depth.

2. THEY SYSTEMATICALLY EXPOSE STUDENTS TO RIVAL POSITIONS ABOUT WHICH THEY MUST MAKE INFORMED JUDGMENTS.

Argument-based courses systematically expose students to rival positions about which they must form judgments. Through repeated exploration of rival positions on a series of big questions, students see historical debate modeled in way that shatters any expectation that historical knowledge is clear-cut and revealed by authority. Students are thus confronted with the inescapable necessity to engage, consider, and ultimately evaluate the merits of a variety of perspectives.

3. THEY ASK STUDENTS TO JUDGE THE RELATIVE MERITS OF RIVAL POSITIONS ON BASIS OF HISTORICAL EVIDENCE.

To participate in historical argument, students must understand historical argument as more than a matter of mere opinion. For this to happen, students must learn to employ evidence as the basis for evaluating historical claims. Through being repeatedly asked to judge the relative merits of rival positions on the basis of evidence, students learnlearn to see the relationship between historical evidence and historical assertions.

4. THEY REQUIRE STUDENTS TO DEVELOP THEIR OWN POSITIONS FOR WHICH THEY MUST ARGUE ON THE BASIS OF HISTORICAL EVIDENCE.

In an argument-based course, the ultimate aspiration should be for students to bring their own voices to bear on historical discourse in a way that is thoroughly grounded in evidence. Students must therefore have the opportunity to argue for their own positions. Such positions may parallel or synthesize those of the scholars with which they have engaged in the course or they may be original. In either case, though, students must practice applying disciplinary standards of evidence.

Learning to argue about history is, above all, a process that requires students to develop new skills, dispositions, and habits of mind. Students develop these attributes through the act of arguing in a supportive environment where the instructor provides guidance and feedback. The instructor is also responsible for providing students with the background, context, and in-depth materials necessary both to fully understand and appreciate each big question and to serve as the body of evidence that forms the basis for judgments and arguments. While argument-based courses eschew any attempt to provide comprehensive coverage, they ask students to think deeply about a smaller number of historical questions—and in the process of arguing about the selected questions, students will develop significant content knowledge in the areas emphasized.

While a number of textbooks and readers in American history incorporate elements of historical argumentation, there are no published materials available that are specifically designed to support an argument-based course. *Debating American History* consists of a series of modular units, each focused on a specific topic and question in American history that will support all four characteristics of an argument-based course noted previously. Instructors will select units that support their overall course design, perhaps incorporating one or two modules into an existing course or structuring an entire course around three to five such units. (Instructors, of course, are free to supplement the modular units with other materials of their choosing, such as additional primary documents, secondary articles, multimedia materials, and book chapters.) By focusing on a limited number of topics, students will be able to engage in in-depth historical argumentation, including consideration of multiple positions and substantial bodies of evidence.

Each unit has the following elements:

1. THE BIG QUESTION

A brief narrative introduction that poses the central question of the unit and provides general background.

2. HISTORIANS' CONVERSATIONS

This section establishes the debate by providing two or three original essays that present distinct and competing scholarly positions on the Big Question. While these essays make occasional reference to major scholars in the field, they are not intended to provide historiographical overviews but rather to provide models of historical argumentation through the presentation and analysis of evidence.

3. DEBATING THE QUESTION

Each module includes a variety of materials containing evidence for students to use to evaluate the various positions and develop a position of their own. Materials may include primary source documents, images, a timeline, maps, or brief secondary sources. The specific materials vary depending on the nature of the question. Some modules include detailed case studies that focus on a particular facet of the Big Question.

For example, one module that we have developed for an early American history course focuses on the following Big Question: "How were the English able to displace the thriving Powhatan people from their Chesapeake homelands in the seventeenth century?" The Historians' Conversations section includes two essays: "Position #1: The Overwhelming Advantages of the English"; and "Position #2: Strategic Mistakes of the Powhatans." The unit materials allow students to undertake a guided exploration of both Powhatan and English motivations and strategies. The materials include two case studies that serve specific pedagogical purposes. The first case study asks the question, "Did Pocahontas Rescue John Smith from Execution?" Answering this question requires grappling with the nature of primary sources and weighing additional evidence from secondary sources;

given historians' confidence that Powhatan did adopt Smith during his captivity, the case study also raises important questions about Powhatan strategy. The second case study focuses on the 1622 surprise attack that the Powhatans (led by Opechancanough) launched against the English, posing the question, "What Was the Strategy behind the 1622 Powhatan Surprise Attack?" Students wrestle with a number of scholarly perspectives regarding Opechancanough's purpose and the effectiveness of his strategy. Overall, this unit introduces students to the use of primary sources and the process of weighing different historical interpretations. Because of Disney's 1995 film *Pocahontas*, many students begin the unit thinking that they already know about the contact between the Powhatans and the English; many of them also savor the chance to bring critical, historical thinking to bear on this subject, and doing so deepens their understanding of how American Indians responded to European colonization.

Along similar lines, the Big Question for a module on the Gilded Age asks, "Why Was Industrialization in the Late Nineteenth Century Accompanied by Such Great Social and Political Turmoil?" The materials provided allow students to explore the labor conflicts of the period as well as the Populist revolt and to draw conclusions regarding the underlying causes of the social and political upheavals. Primary sources allow students to delve into labor conflicts from the perspectives of both the workers and management and to explore both Populist and anti-Populist perspectives. Three short case studies allow students to examine specific instances of social conflict in depth. A body of economic data from the late nineteenth century is also included.

Many history instructors, when presented with the argument-based model, find its goals to be compelling, but they fear that it is overly ambitious—that introductory-level students will be incapable of engaging in historical thinking at an acceptable level. But, we must ask, how well do students learn under the coverage model? Student performance varies in an argument-based course, but it varies widely in a coverage-based course as well. In our experience, most undergraduate students are capable of achieving a basic-level competence at identifying and evaluating historical interpretations and using primary and secondary sources as evidence to make basic historical arguments. We not only have evidence of this success in the form of our own grade books, but we have studied our students' learning to document the success of our approach.[11] Students can indeed learn how to think like historians at a novice level, and in doing so they will gain both an appreciation for the discipline and develop a set of critical skills and dispositions that will contribute to their overall higher education. For this to happen, however, a course must be "backward designed" to promote and develop historical thinking. As historian Lawrence Gipson (Wabash College) asked in a 1916 AHA discussion, "Will the student catch 'historical-mindedness' from his instructor like the mumps?"[12] The answer, clearly, is "no."

In addition to the modular units focused on big questions, instructors will also be provided with a brief instructors' manual, entitled "Developing an Argument-Based Course."

---

11   See Sipress, "Why Students Don't Get Evidence," and Voelker, "Assessing Student Understanding."
12   Lawrence H. Gipson, "Method of the Elementary Course in the Small College," *The History Teacher's Magazine* 8 (April 1917), 128. (The conference discussion took place in 1916.)

This volume will provide instructors with guidance and advice on course development, as well as with sample in-class exercises and assessments. Additionally, each module includes an Instructor's Manual. Together, these resources will assist instructors with the process of creating an argument-based course, whether for a relatively small class at a liberal arts college or for a large class of students at a university. These resources can be used in both face-to-face and online courses.

The purpose of *Debating American History* is to provide instructors with both the resources and strategies that they will need to design such a course. This textbook alternative leaves plenty of room for instructor flexibility; and it requires instructors to carefully choose, organize, and introduce the readings to students, as well as to coach students through the process of thinking historically, even as they deepen their knowledge and understanding of particular eras and topics.

Joel M. Sipress
Professor of History,
University of Wisconsin-Superior

David J. Voelker
Associate Professor of Humanities and History,
University of Wisconsin-Green Bay

DEBATING AMERICAN HISTORY

THE POWHATANS AND THE ENGLISH
IN THE SEVENTEENTH-CENTURY CHESAPEAKE

THE BIG QUESTION

HOW WERE THE ENGLISH ABLE TO DISPLACE THE THRIVING POWHATAN PEOPLE FROM THEIR CHESAPEAKE HOMELANDS IN THE SEVENTEENTH CENTURY?

The ends of this voyage are these: 1. To plant the Christian religion. 2. To trafficke [trade]. 3. To conquer. Or, to doe all three.

—RICHARD HAKLUYT, THE ELDER, *Inducements to the Liking of the Voyage Intended Towards Virginia* (1585)

What will it availe you to take that by force you may quickly have by love, or to destroy them that provide you food. What can you get by warre, when we can hide our provisions and fly to the woods? Whereby you must famish by wronging us your friends. . . . Thinke you I am so simple, not to know it is better to eate good meate, lye well, and sleepe quietly with my women and children, laugh and be merry with you, have copper, hatchets, or what I want being your friend: then be forced to flie from all, to lie cold in the woods, feede upon Acornes, rootes, and such trash, and be so hunted by you[?] . . . Let this therefore assure you of our loves, and every yeare our friendly trade shall furnish you with Corne; and now also, if you would come in friendly manner to see us, and not thus with your guns and swords as to invade your foes.

—SPEECH ATTRIBUTED TO CHIEF POWHATAN FROM JOHN SMITH'S *Generall Historie of Virginia* (1624)

On March 22, 1622, the Powhatan Indians of **Tsenacommacah**, the "densely inhabited land" surrounding the Chesapeake Bay, launched a massive surprise attack against the English colonists who had been spreading across the region since the 1607 founding of Jamestown. On that day, nearly 350 of the almost 1,250 English settlers of the Virginia Colony were killed. The dead included men, women, and children. Among them was George Thorpe, who had led efforts to Christianize the Powhatans in hope of establishing a basis for peace. Hundreds more English died of famine and disease over the following winter, as the Powhatans had attacked before spring planting and kept the English confined to defensible areas. Largely as a result of this attack, within three years, nearly 70% of the colonists perished.[1]

This surprise attack, which the English called a "massacre," followed several years of relative peace between the English settlers and their Powhatan neighbors. Indeed, it seemed possible for a time that the English and the Powhatans had worked out a means of coexistence. By the middle of the 1610s, both **Werowance** (or Chief) **Powhatan** (the paramount chieftain over about thirty tribal communities in the region; also known by his personal name, **Wahunsenaca**) and his daughter Pocahontas (who as an adult became known among her people as **Matoaka**) seemed committed to peace. After the 1614 marriage of John Rolfe and Pocahontas, who took the Christian name Rebecca, several Powhatan families began dwelling among the English. **Opechancanough** (Powhatan's brother or cousin, who eventually became paramount chief after Powhatan died in 1618) had agreed to allow Christian proselytization among his people in exchange for Powhatan warriors gaining access to and training in the use of English muskets. To be sure, the Virginia Colony was hardly free from conflict, and both Powhatans and English lost many lives to disease in the several years before 1622. It seemed plausible, though, that the Powhatans might strategically accommodate to English culture and that the worst of the violence between the two groups might be over.

The 1622 attack marked the end of any such integration of Powhatan and English societies and perhaps showed that such integration was not possible on terms that either party could accept. Despite the loss of over one-fourth of their population on a single day, the English did not relinquish their hold on the Chesapeake, where they were just beginning to reap substantial profits by growing tobacco for export. In fact, the surprise attack backfired for the Powhatans because it reinforced the common and ethnocentric notion among the English that the Native people were untrustworthy savages. The English thus felt justified in waging a fierce war against the Powhatans. As colonial official Edward Waterhouse wrote in 1622, "We . . . may now by right of war, and law of nations, invade the country, and destroy them who sought to destroy us; whereby we shall enjoy their cultivated places." Meeting the duplicity of the surprise attack with duplicity of their own, the English poisoned and killed a number of Powhatans at a fraudulent peace conference. The English, however, did not attempt to eradicate the Powhatans altogether: they recognized that they needed the Powhatans as trading partners and military allies. Nevertheless, in the years after 1622, the colony's expansion continued despite a second devastating surprise attack by the Powhatans in 1644. By mid-century, the English were growing tobacco on the most valuable lands in the region; and by the century's end, the remaining Powhatans were confined to small reservations.

When English colonizers arrived in the Chesapeake Bay in 1607, the region was inhabited by tens of thousands of Native people. The English settlement of Jamestown began badly: a combination of starvation, disease, and warfare led to an estimated 80% mortality rate over the first ten years. Moreover, the two major surprise attacks orchestrated

---

1   Brendan Wolfe, "The Virginia Company of London," *Encyclopedia Virginia* (Virginia Foundation for the Humanities), May 23, 2013, http://www.encyclopediavirginia.org/Virginia_Company_of_London#start_entry. Accessed September 11, 2013.

by the Powhatans in 1622 and 1644 helped keep the English population smaller than the Powhatans' for several decades. Nonetheless, the English were able to dominate the region within a matter of decades. How were the English able to displace the thriving Powhatan people from their Chesapeake homelands in the seventeenth century?

The Powhatans were not naïve about the potential dangers posed by these strangers who came from across the sea. In fact, the Powhatans had weathered a number of encounters with Spanish, French, and English wayfarers. Within living memory, the Spanish had attempted to establish a Jesuit mission (known as **Ajacán**) in the heart of Tsenacommacah. In 1561, Spanish marauders had kidnapped two boys from the region. Nearly a decade later, one of the two boys, Paquiquineo, by then a young man, returned to Tsenacommacah with a small company of Jesuit missionaries (after being taken to both Spain and Mexico City). The information he shared led his people to eradicate the mission and kill its inhabitants, sparing only a young boy. The Spanish reciprocated this violence through a raid on Tsenacommacah the next year. Although they recovered the Spanish boy, they were unable to locate Paquiquineo (known to them as Don Luís de Velasco). There were more kidnappings perpetrated by the Spanish in the following decade. It is not certain that Paquiquineo survived until the founding of Jamestown, but surely his story did—including the memory of the punitive strike that the Spanish made after the destruction of the mission.[2] Some historians have speculated that one of Chief Powhatan's motives for establishing himself as paramount chief over much of Tsenacommacah was to defend it against future Spanish invasions. By 1600, Powhatan's chiefdom incorporated about thirty tribes and approximately 15,000 of the estimated 30,000 inhabitants of the bay region. (See Maps 1 and 2.)

A decade following the destruction of Ajacán, the English had twice attempted to establish a settlement at Roanoke Island, about fifty miles south of the mouth of the Chesapeake Bay. During the first attempt to settle Roanoke Island in 1585, a number of settlers had resided for months on the mainland near the Chesapeake. By the following spring, the island colony was abandoned after significant violence had broken out between the settlers and the Roanoke Indians, in large part because of the English demand for food—a pattern that would be repeated in Jamestown two decades later. A second attempt to settle Roanoke in 1587 also ended in failure, this time with the colonists disappearing altogether. Although the fate of these "Lost Colonists" has been much debated, they may well have sought refuge or been taken as prisoners on the mainland. One interesting possibility is that they were adopted by a tribe known as the Chesapeake Indians, which Powhatan took the highly unusual step of ordering eradicated either just before or just after the arrival of the Jamestown settlers.[3] These various incidents serve as a reminder that political threats and conflicts, both with European empires and Native rivals, were part of the world that the Powhatans inhabited.

---

2   Karen O. Kupperman, *The Jamestown Project* (Cambridge, MA: Harvard University Press, 2007), 103–105; Helen C. Rountree, *Pocahontas, Powhatan, and Opechancanough: Three Indian Lives Changed by Jamestown* (Charlottesville: University of Virginia Press, 2006), 26–29.

3   Kupperman, *Jamestown Project*, 32, 95.

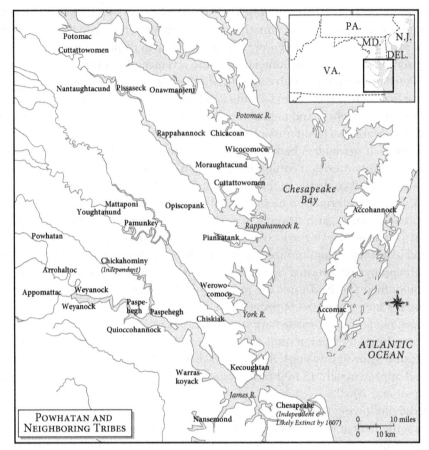

MAP 1. POWHATAN AND NEIGHBORING TRIBES
Sources: Frederic W. Gleach, *Powhatan's World and Colonial Virginia: A Conflict of Cultures*
(Lincoln: University of Nebraska Press, 1997), 23; Helen C. Rountree, *Pocahontas,
Powhatan, Opechancanough: Three Indian Lives Changed by Jamestown* (Charlottesville:
University of Virginia Press, 2006), 40; and Nell Marion Nugent, *Cavaliers and Pioneers:
Abstracts of Virginia Land Patents and Grants, 1623–1800*, Vol. 1 (Richmond: Press of the
Dietz Print Co., 1934), front endsheet.

The English and Powhatans thus had good reasons to be wary of one another upon
the arrival of the English at Tsenacommacah in late April 1607 to found Jamestown. The
English were also concerned about possible attacks by the French or the Spanish, the latter
of whom laid claim to the region and had a settlement at St. Augustine, Florida, dating
back to 1565. This fear largely explains why the English sailed up the newly dubbed James
River to establish their colony on a peninsula that seasonally became a small island: they
wanted to be able to see their enemies coming. The reason the area was uninhabited, however, was because it was swampy and insect ridden. Worse, the available water was often
brackish, tainted by seawater from the bay. The site may have been relatively secure, but it
was also terribly unhealthy.

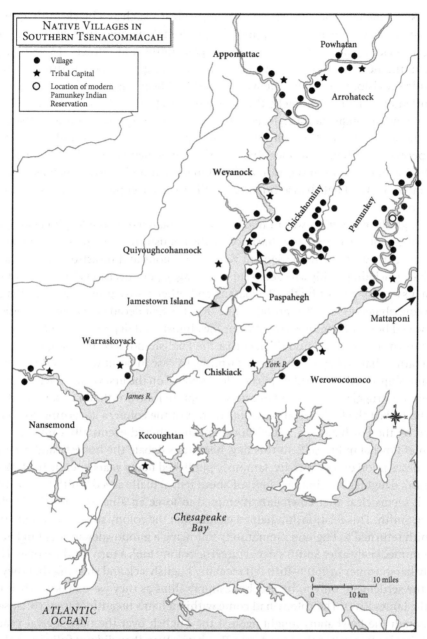

MAP 2. NATIVE VILLAGES IN SOUTHERN TSENACOMMACAH, 1607
Source: Helen C. Rountree, *Pocahontas, Powhatan, Opechancanough: Three Indian Lives Changed by Jamestown* (Charlottesville: University of Virginia Press, 2006), 54.

The early settlers were dominated neither by soldiers nor farmers but by a mixture of unskilled workers and skilled craftsmen. Among the original 104 colonists were both men and boys but no women, which no doubt made a strange appearance to the Powhatans.

The craftsmen included personnel essential to survival—such as a blacksmith, gunsmith, and surgeon—as well as men to support the profit-making objectives of the colony: including a tobacco pipe-maker, a jeweler, and goldsmiths and refiners. (A second group of settlers the next year included German and Polish glassmakers.) Although the settlers made provisions to defend themselves and had been instructed to "take great care not to offend the naturals [namely, the Native peoples]," they did not plan to seize large swaths of land in conquistador style. Nor did they plan to grow much food for themselves. Rather, the settlers hoped through some combination of awe and intimidation to subdue Native peoples as tributaries—meaning that the Native peoples would provide food and animal skins in return for protection and manufactured trade goods, such as glass beads and metal tools. The English also hoped mightily to discover precious metals and a water passage to Asia.

Although the expedition was in many ways well planned by the Virginia Company of London, the joint-stock company chartered by the English crown in 1606 that operated the colony, the early years of the settlement were tumultuous and disastrous. A combination of bad luck (including a shipwrecked resupply voyage), poor decisions (the siting of Jamestown in a swamp), attacks by the Powhatans and other Native groups, and deaths due to disease contributed to an 80% mortality rate over the first decade of settlement. Additionally, repeated bouts of famine resulted from the almost total dependence of the English on Native-grown corn for food and the fact that the English indulged their impulse to search for gold rather than to begin subsistence farming. (A case in point was the effort exerted to gather and ship a load of worthless pyrite, "fool's gold," on the first voyage back to England.)

Amid the struggle to establish Jamestown, Captain John Smith (an experienced adventurer who lacked the high social status of the rest of the colony's governing council) was captured by the Powhatan war chief Opechancanough and eventually came face to face with Chief Powhatan himself. To this day, historians debate the honesty and accuracy of Smith's description of his captivity, famously published many years later in 1624. Whether Powhatan's daughter Pocahontas, a girl of about ten, actually saved Smith from execution or not, it seems clear that Powhatan attempted to forge an alliance with the English by adopting Smith. This relationship helped ensure that the colony survived, despite the fact that Smith returned to England prematurely following a gunpowder accident in late 1609. Almost immediately after Smith's departure, the colony took a turn for the worse. The particularly harsh winter in 1609–1610 left so many English sick and starving that they abandoned the settlement, only to be met by resupply ships as they were making their escape down the James River. The colony had come within a hair's breadth of total collapse.

Although the Powhatans fought against the English over the next several years in a conflict that is often called the First Anglo-Powhatan War, they did not fully press their advantage. In fact, between 1610 and the spring of 1614, it was the English who went on the offensive to seize both food and land. In 1613, Captain Samuel Argall captured Pocahontas. The following April, after a year in captivity, she converted to Christianity and married the Englishman John Rolfe. This diplomatic marriage concluded the war, but not necessarily to the benefit of the Powhatans. With the end of the conflict, some Powhatans began to live with the English and were taught about Christianity. Meanwhile, Rolfe learned the techniques necessary to grow and cure tobacco, probably with help from his wife and members of her family. Thus, Powhatan's decision to make peace in 1614 had profound

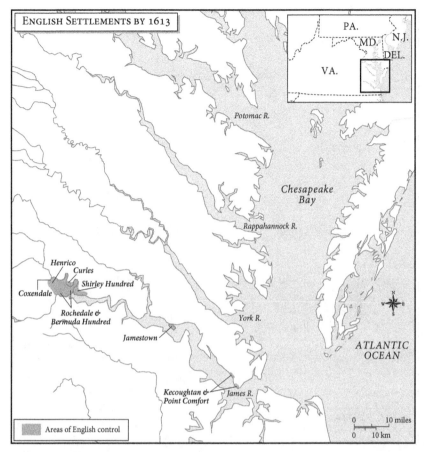

MAP 3. ENGLISH SETTLEMENTS TO 1613
Sources: Frederic W. Gleach, *Powhatan's World and Colonial Virginia: A Conflict of Cultures*
(Lincoln: University of Nebraska Press, 1997), 134; and Nell Marion Nugent, *Cavaliers
and Pioneers: Abstracts of Virginia Land Patents and Grants, 1623–1800*, Vol. 1 (Richmond:
Press of the Dietz Print Co., 1934), front endsheet.

consequences. Most notably, the advent of English tobacco cultivation set the colony on a
road to profitability and unleashed a profound hunger for fertile land among the English.
(See Map 3 for the location of English settlements as of 1613.)

Whether Pocahontas realized it or not, her 1616 voyage to London with her husband,
her young son Thomas, and an entourage of her people was intended to boost the prospects of the Virginia Company by attracting additional investors and settlers. Traveling
with Pocahontas was the Powhatan "priest" or medicine person, **Uttamatomakkin** (or
Tomocomo), who was apparently asked by Powhatan to gather intelligence about the
English homeland. Neither Pocahontas, who died suddenly from illness as the travelers
were returning home, nor her son Thomas, who was left in the care of John's brother, made
the return trip to Tsenacommacah in 1617.[4]

---

4   Camilla Townsend, *Pocahontas and the Powhatan Dilemma* (New York: Hill & Wang, 2005), 168–175.

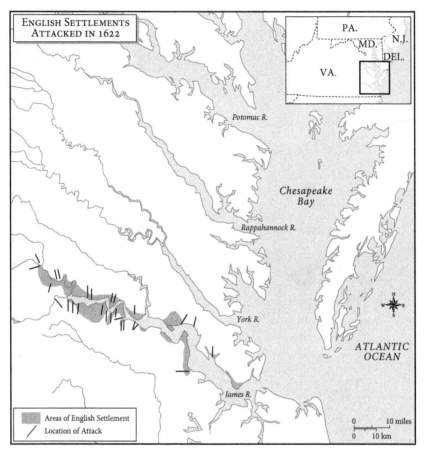

MAP 4. ENGLISH SETTLEMENTS AND LOCATIONS ATTACKED IN 1622
Sources: Frederic W. Gleach, *Powhatan's World and Colonial Virginia: A Conflict of Cultures*
(Lincoln: University of Nebraska Press, 1997), 150; and Nell Marion Nugent, *Cavaliers
and Pioneers: Abstracts of Virginia Land Patents and Grants, 1623–1800*, Vol. 1 (Richmond:
Press of the Dietz Print Co., 1934), 224.

After the death of Pocahontas, the aging Powhatan ceded power to two successors,
including Opechancanough. With the success of tobacco as a cash crop, the relationship
between the Powhatans and the English continued to deteriorate. By 1622, the English
had established almost three dozen small settlements in addition to Jamestown.[5] (See
Map 4 for English settlements in 1622.) It was within this context that the Powhatans
launched their deadly surprise attack. After years of ongoing conflict (primarily English
raids to destroy Powhatan food supplies), somewhat peaceful relations were reestab-
lished in 1630s, only to lead to continued loss of land and autonomy for the Powhatans.[6]

---

5   Rountree, *Pocahontas, Powhatan, and Opechancanough*, 188.
6   Frederic W. Gleach, *Powhatan's World and Colonial Virginia: A Conflict of Cultures* (Lincoln: University of
Nebraska Press, 1997), 159–161.

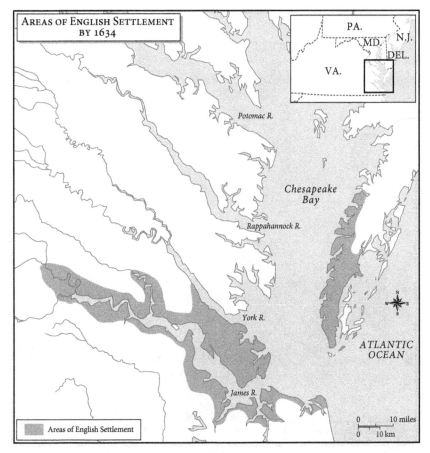

MAP 5. AREAS OF ENGLISH SETTLEMENT BY 1634
Sources: Frederic W. Gleach, *Powhatan's World and Colonial Virginia: A Conflict of Cultures* (Lincoln: University of Nebraska Press, 1997), 170; and Nell Marion Nugent, *Cavaliers and Pioneers: Abstracts of Virginia Land Patents and Grants, 1623–1800*, Vol. 1 (Richmond: Press of the Dietz Print Co., 1934), rear endsheet.

The Virginia Company lost its charter in 1624, but the colony's population continued to grow over the next several decades. (See Map 5 for English settlements in 1634 and Map 6 for English settlements in 1652.) A key factor in attracting immigrants was a "headright" system that offered land to settlers who could pay for the passage of themselves (with bonuses for family members and servants) and the promise of free land for indentured servants who survived the typical five- to seven-year period of servitude required to pay for their passage across the Atlantic. These systems of land distribution and labor, along with the booming export market for tobacco, allowed the English settlement to thrive. (Although a small number of African servants arrived during the early decades of the colony, enslaved Africans did not become a dominant source of labor until the 1680s and 1690s.)

As the English continued to expand their presence in Tsenacommacah, the Powhatans made one final attempt to contain them. On April 18, 1644, the Powhatans launched a second major surprise strike against the English, killing even more settlers than they had

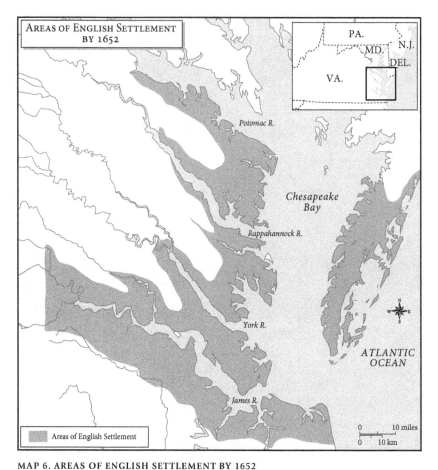

MAP 6. AREAS OF ENGLISH SETTLEMENT BY 1652
Sources: Frederic W. Gleach, *Powhatan's World and Colonial Virginia: A Conflict of Cultures*
(Lincoln: University of Nebraska Press, 1997), 187; and Nell Marion Nugent, *Cavaliers
and Pioneers: Abstracts of Virginia Land Patents and Grants, 1623–1800*, Vol. 1 (Richmond:
Press of the Dietz Print Co., 1934), rear endsheet.

in the 1622 attack. Two years later, the English captured the very elderly Opechancanough,
who was soon murdered in captivity. With Opechancanough's death, the Powhatan coalition effectively came to an end. In the treaty that concluded this third major conflict
between the Powhatans and English, the Powhatans forfeited the land between the James
and York rivers and became subordinates under English protection.

This protection did little good for the surviving Powhatans when a group of settlers
led by Nathaniel Bacon rose in rebellion in 1676. Bacon's followers were discontented
small farmers and landless men who were frustrated by high taxes, falling tobacco prices,
and declining availability of land. They both attacked the colony's government (burning Jamestown) and made indiscriminate war against Native peoples on the frontiers and
inside the established boundaries of the colony. The Treaty of Middle Plantation, which
was signed by the **Pamunkey** "Queen" Cockacoeske (a relative of Powhatan and Opechancanough) and other tribal chiefs, established what amounted to reservation lands for the
"several scattered Nations" that once made up the Powhatan coalition. Tributaries on their

own homelands, the Powhatans nonetheless endured. (Both the **Mattaponi** and Pamunkey tribes, which were part of the **Powhatan chiefdom**, maintain small reservations in Virginia to this day. Eleven tribes are recognized by the state of Virginia. Several of the tribes worked for many years to secure official recognition of the federal government. In 2015, the Pamunkey tribe was granted federal recognition; and in 2018, the Chickahominy, Eastern Chickahominy, Upper Mattaponi, Rappahannock, Monacan, and Nansemond tribes were also recognized and became eligible for federal funding and protection.)

The subordination of the Powhatans set the stage for the Chesapeake Bay region and the larger Virginia Colony to be transformed by English settlement, tobacco cultivation, and the expanded use of enslaved Africans. By the late 1600s, there were probably more English settlers in eastern Virginia than there had been Native people at the time of Jamestown's founding, and there were already nearly as many African slaves as there were Native people living in the Chesapeake region. Population estimates for 1745 suggest the extent of this transformation: at that time, the Chesapeake region of Virginia was home to 600 Native people, nearly 150,000 English settlers, and about 85,000 African and African American slaves.[7]

In hindsight, it seems possible the Powhatans could have eradicated the Jamestown settlement during its early years—just as they had Ajacán a few decades earlier—thus nipping the English threat in the bud, at least for the time being. As historians in recent decades have attempted to better understand the Powhatan perspective, they have puzzled over the strategies that Chief Powhatan and his successor Opechancanough used to cope with the founding of Jamestown. As J. Frederick Fausz has asked, "Why did Powhatan and his people allow Jamestown to survive?"[8]

Two episodes from the history of Powhatan–English interaction stand out as particularly important for casting light on the Powhatan strategy. First, there is the question of how Chief Powhatan handled the opportunity offered by the capture of Captain John Smith, who turned out to be so pivotal in the survival of the colony during its first years. Did Powhatan in fact spare Smith's life in deference to the wishes of his ten-year-old daughter Pocahontas? Or was there some other strategy at work? Along similar lines, why did Powhatan opt not to destroy the colony after the winter of 1609–1610, when it was in its most vulnerable state?

Second, there is the question of the strategic intention and effectiveness of the attacks launched by Opechancanough in 1622 and 1644. Despite the damage they inflicted, these assaults seemed only to strengthen English resolve. While these two incidents stand out, other scholars draw attention to the larger context of the Virginia Colony, emphasizing the importance of factors such as disease and technology that tended to give the English advantages over the long term.

The Virginia Colony was the first enduring English settlement in mainland North America, and in many ways it set precedents for English colonization. By exploring the historical debate over its creation, we can better understand both the English approach to colonization and the plight of Native American tribal nations as they struggled to respond to the arrival

---

7   Peter Wallenstein, *Cradle of America: Four Centuries of Virginia History* (Lawrence: University Press of Kansas, 2007), 38.

8   J. Frederick Fausz, "The Invasion of Virginia: Indians, Colonialism, and the Conquest of Cant: A Review Essay on Anglo-Indian Relations in the Chesapeake," *Virginia Magazine of History and Biography* 95 (April 1987): 133–156; see 145.

of these strangers with their dreadful pathogens and powerful technologies. By studying the demise of the Powhatan chiefdom, we can better understand how English modes of interacting with Native people allowed them to achieve dominance. We can also learn about how tribal nations managed to survive the colonial period through some combination of resistance and strategic accommodation. Additionally, we can gain insight into the mythology that the English colonizers and later European Americans developed regarding Pocahontas and other allegedly sympathetic Native people who supposedly assisted the colonizers.

There are, however, significant challenges to studying and understanding the interaction of Native Americans and European colonizers during this period. As just hinted at, the English and Anglo-Americans who seized North America largely controlled the stories told about their conquest, whether through historical monuments (such as the multiple depictions of Pocahontas in the United States Capitol building that were installed in the nineteenth century) or through the mass media of more recent times. Depictions of Native Americans in film and television have generated a whole raft of stereotypes and assumptions that can impede historical understanding. Perhaps even more challenging is the fact that virtually all of the written documentation from this period comes from the English colonizers. Most of these documents present the English perspective exclusively; if they do present the Powhatan perspective, they often do so largely to bolster their own agendas—as John Smith did when he wrote about his experiences with the Powhatans in Virginia.

Historians attempt to account for the limited perspectives in documentary sources in a number of ways. First, they read primary documents critically, keeping in mind the biases of the English. When reading John Smith's accounts of his dealing with Powhatan and Pocahontas, for example, it is important to keep in mind that he had his own reasons for telling these stories and casting them as he did. Second, historians contextualize the sources with knowledge about Native cultures from the time, gleaned by historical anthropologists and other scholars. For example, scholar Helen Rountree (cited numerous times in the essays that follow), has carried out a comprehensive investigation of Powhatan culture to understand their decisions within the context of their own culture. We thus know, for instance, that the Powhatans used intermarriage to forge kinship relationships and seal alliances with former rivals or enemies, which gives us an important context for understanding Pocahontas's marriage to John Rolfe. Third, historians can take into account the narratives that have been passed down by Native people from one generation to the next in a form of knowledge transmission known as the oral tradition. In many cases, the oral tradition has not been recorded in print form and is not easily accessible; fortunately, however, Custalow Linwood and Angela L. Daniel of the Mattaponi tribe (which was part of the Powhatan chiefdom) have published the oral tradition, as preserved among the Mattaponi people, regarding the confrontation of the Powhatans and English in the seventeenth century.[9]

Taking into account not only the English documentary record but also what we know about Powhatan culture, we can confront this historical puzzle. The Powhatans certainly had the advantage of numbers and military strength over the English at least as late as 1610. How, then, were the English able to displace the thriving Powhatan people from their Chesapeake homelands in the seventeenth century?

---

9   Linwood "Little Bear" Custalow and Angela L. Daniel "Little Star," *The True Story of Pocahontas: The Other Side of History* (Golden, CO: Fulcrum Publishing, 2007).

GLOSSARY

AJACÁN: A Spanish Jesuit mission in the Chesapeake region that existed briefly from September 1570 to February 1571. The mission was established with the cooperation of a Native man named Paquiquineo, who took the name Don Luís de Velasco while he was in the custody of the Spanish. The Spanish had likely kidnapped Paquiquineo about a decade early; and after this, he had traveled under Spanish custody to Spain, Mexico, and Cuba. Paquiquineo apparently convinced his people, upon returning to his Chesapeake homeland with several Jesuits, that the missionary settlement should be destroyed and the priests killed. He participated in the assault himself.

MATOAKA: The adult name of Pocahontas. After her baptism and marriage in 1614, she was also known by the name Rebecca Rolfe.

MATTAPONI: One of the primary tribes of the Powhatan chiefdom. According to Mattaponi oral tradition, Pocahontas's mother was a member of this tribe.[10]

OPECHANCANOUGH (C. 1550s–1646): Opechancanough was a close relative of Chief Powhatan—likely a brother, half-brother, or cousin. At the time of the English founding of Jamestown in 1607, Opechancanough served as war chief of the Powhatans, under Chief Powhatan's leadership. Within a year or so after Chief Powhatan's death in 1618, Opechancanough assumed the position of paramount (or overarching) chief of the Powhatan alliance. He coordinated major surprise attacks against the English in 1622 and 1644. He was murdered while being held captive by the English in 1646.

PAMUNKEY: The primary tribe of the Powhatan chiefdom. Both Powhatan and Opechancanough were of the Pamunkey tribe.

POWHATAN CHIEFDOM: The Powhatan chiefdom was an alliance of approximately thirty tribes of the southern half of the Chesapeake Bay region. At the time of the English arrival in 1607, the chiefdom was led by Werowance Powhatan.

POWHATAN (C. 1550–1618): Werowance Powhatan was the paramount or overarching chief of the Powhatan alliance, which he had created or at least substantially expanded to encompass about thirty tribes during the couple of decades before the establishment of the Jamestown colony in 1607. Also known by his personal name of Wahunsenaca (or Wahunsonacock), Powhatan was the father of Pocahontas. After his death in 1618, he was eventually succeeded by his brother (or cousin) Opechancanough as paramount chief.

QUIAKROS: The title for Powhatan medicine people, who served as healers, spiritual leaders, and political advisers. Powhatan chiefs were known to consult regularly with the quiakros and to abide by their visions and prophecies. The English sometimes referred to the quiakros as "priests" because of their spiritual and ceremonial leadership.

TSENACOMMACAH: Also spelled Tsenacomoco, this word refers to approximately the southern half of the Chesapeake Bay area. The word can also refer to the Powhatan chiefdom that occupied this region. In the Powhatan language, Tsenacommacah is thought to mean "densely inhabited area." Indeed, the region was home to an estimated 15,000

---

10   See Linwood "Little Bear" Custalow and Angela L. Daniel "Little Star," *The True Story of Pocahontas: The Other Side of History*, Golden, CO: Fulcrum Publishing, 2007.

Native people at the time of the English founding of Jamestown in 1607.

UTTAMATOMAKKIN: Also known as Tomocomo, Uttamatomakkin was a Powhatan medicine person (or "priest," as the English called him) who traveled to England as part of Pocahontas's entourage in 1616–1617. Having been assigned to collect intelligence about the English, Uttamatomakkin returned home in 1617 with both a negative view of the English and sobering news about the strength of their population and resources—information that no doubt informed Opechancanough's strategies for dealing with the English colonizers over the decades to come.

WAHUNSENACA: See Powhatan.

WEROWANCE: The title used for tribal chiefs in the Chesapeake Bay region. There are a number of alternate spellings, including weroance.

TIMELINE

1561	1607 (May)	1609–1610 (Winter)
Kidnapping of Paquiquineo (aka, Don Luís de Velasco)	First group of 105 settlers establish Jamestown	Jamestown colonists suffer through "Starving Time"
c. 1570s	**1607 (December)**	**1610 (May)**
Werowance Powhatan begins consolidating chiefdom of about 30 tribes in Tsenacommacah	Opechancanough captures Captain John Smith and delivers him to Werowance Powhatan	Lieutenant Governor Thomas Gates arrives to find colony in tatters
1570	**1608 (January)**	**1610 (June)**
Spanish Jesuits return with Don Luís de Velasco to create Ajacán settlement in the Chesapeake Bay region	Resupply ship brings a hundred new settlers to struggling colony	Survivors of harsh winter abandon Jamestown but are met by resupply ship
1571	**1608 (September)**	**1612**
Native people of Tsenacommacah destroy Ajacán	Captain John Smith begins term as President of Jamestown	John Rolfe produces his first small tobacco crop for shipment to England
1572	**1609 (July)**	**1613 (April)**
Spanish avenge deaths of Ajacán missionaries and recover surviving Spanish boy	Resupply flagship *Sea Venture* shipwrecked at Bermuda	Pocahontas, daughter of Werowance Powhatan, captured by Captain Samuel Argall
1585	**1609 (Summer)**	**1614 (April)**
First unsuccessful English attempt to settle Roanoke Island	First Anglo-Powhatan War begins as English fight to obtain food from the Powhatan people	Pocahontas, having been baptized and taken the name Rebecca, marries John Rolfe; First Anglo-Powhatan War ends
1587	**1609 (October)**	**1614**
Second unsuccessful English attempt to settle Roanoke Island	Captain John Smith departs for England after accidental injury	English create three settlements in addition to Jamestown

Sources:

Encyclopedia Virginia, http://encyclopediavirginia.org

"History Timeline," *Jamestown Rediscovery: Historic Jamestowne*, at https://historicjamestowne.org/history/history-timeline/. Accessed January 31, 2019.

"Timeline," *Virtual Jamestown*, at http://www.virtualjamestown.org/timeline2.html. Accessed September 25, 2013.

1615 Pocahontas (Rebecca Rolfe) gives birth to Thomas Rolfe	**1619** Second significant bout of epidemic disease (since English arrival) afflicts Powhatans	**1640** Virginia Assembly passes legislation regarding African slaves
1616 John, Pocahontas (Rebecca), and Thomas Rolfe travel to England with several Powhatan people in their entourage and a shipment of tobacco	**c. 1620** Opechancanough allows some Powhatans to live with the English and learn about Christianity in return for Powhatan warriors gaining firearm training	**1644 (April 18)** Powhatans launch a second major surprise attack against the English, killing nearly 500
1617 (March) Pocahontas (Rebecca Rolfe) dies in England; John Rolfe leaves their son with family in England	**1621** Nemattanew ("Jack of the Feathers") kills several Englishmen	**1646 (October)** Opechancanough is captured and murdered
1617 First significant bout of epidemic disease (since English arrival) afflicts Powhatans	**1622 (March)** English kill Nemattanew in revenge	**1662** Additional legislation on slavery makes enslaved status hereditary through mother
1618 (Spring) Werowance Powhatan dies		
1618 (November) Virginia Company implements "headright" system to distribute land	**1622 (March 22)** Powhatans launch massive surprise attack on the English, killing 347	**1676 (September)** Nathaniel Bacon and followers burn Jamestown
1619 Opechancanough becomes paramount chief of the Powhatans	**1622–1623 (Winter)** Hundreds more Virginia colonists die of famine and disease	**1676 (October)** Nathaniel Bacon dies and his rebellion collapses
1619 The first (known) African slaves arrive in Virginia	**1624** Virginia Company of London loses charter; Virginia becomes a royal colony	**1677** Colonial officials negotiate treaty with indigenous nations of Virginia on behalf of the Crown

HISTORIANS' CONVERSATIONS

POSITION #1—THE OVERWHELMING ADVANTAGES OF THE ENGLISH

When a group of Englishmen representing the Virginia Company of London sailed into Chesapeake Bay in May of 1607, the paramount chief, Werowance Powhatan, had been strengthening his hand in the region for decades. His chiefdom included approximately thirty tribes, and he could count on the support of over 3,000 warriors. By all appearances, the Powhatans had the upper hand over the 104 bedraggled Englishmen who set up camp and hastily constructed a fort on swampy lands within the boundaries of Powhatan's chiefdom of Tsenacommacah. But these appearances are deceptive because they obscure the extent to which the English represented a force beyond the reckoning of the Powhatans. Once the ambitous and determined English established their outpost, there would be no stopping them. For the English carried with them not only deadly weapons and even deadlier diseases but also a set of beliefs and desires that would drive them to colonize all lands and peoples they encountered in America. The Powhatans, moreover, did not know enough about English culture, motives, and resources to justify launching a quick and decisive campaign to evict the strangers from Tsenacommacah. Given what the Powhatans knew and when they knew it, they were unable to mount sufficient resistance in time to stop the English expansion. The English success in conquering the Chesapeake, as in other regions up and down the Atlantic seaboard, rested on the material, technological, economic, biological, and ideological advantages that they held over the continent's indigenous inhabitants.

To be sure, Powhatan and his war chief, Opechancanough, were neither naive nor defenseless. As historian Camilla Townsend has written, Powhatan "knew how to wield power," a fact proven by "His storehouses [that] were full of goods produced by conquered tribes." Although Powhatan's power over his tributaries was far from absolute, he was, by Townsend's account, "a brilliant strategist forging a new political unity."[1] His eradication of the Chesapeake tribe on the basis of a prophecy that emerged from his *quiakros* (medicine people, or "priests," as the English sometimes called them) gives some indication of Powhatan's willingness to use violent force to preserve his power. In addition to being skilled in the arts of leadership, diplomacy, and warfare, Powhatan possessed strategically valuable intelligence regarding the English and other Europeans. His own people and neighboring tribes had encountered bearded, coat-wearing strangers from the sea before, having destroyed a Spanish mission in their vicinity in 1571. Additionally, Powhatan surely knew of the two English attempts to settle Roanoke Island in the 1580s, both of which ended in

---

1   Camilla Townsend, *Pocahontas and the Powhatan Dilemma* (New York: Hill & Wang, 2005), 14.

failure. (The Roanoke colonists did have some contact with the Chesapeake tribe—thus the speculation that they may have sought refuge with them after the second failed attempt to establish a settlement.) There were likely additional undocumented interactions along the shores of the Chesapeake, including various attempts to trade.

All of this is to say that Powhatan was hardly unaware of the possible threat posed by the strangers. Still, as historical anthropologist Helen Rountree has noted, the Powhatans had "met or heard of a very few parties of Europeans in the previous thirty-seven years, and none of those lasted long." The seafaring strangers may have possessed impressive ships, cannons, and armor, but they did not seem especially capable of fending for themselves.[2] In other words, the English did not appear to pose a major threat.

All of Powhatan's political savvy and experience, however, proved ineffective against the English newcomers. Ultimately, the problem was not simply that Powhatan or his successor Opechancanough made strategic errors. The challenges that the Powhatans faced upon the arrival of the English ran much deeper than strategy. As Townsend has eloquently stated: "When the two cultures met and entered a power struggle over land and resources, it would turn out that, unbeknownst to either side, they had been in something like a technological race for centuries. And the cultural heirs of people who had been full-time agriculturalists for eleven thousand years rather than a few hundred had already won."[3] Townsend here applies insights of Jared Diamond, a biologist-turned-geographer-turned-historian who won the Pulitzer Prize for History in 1998 for his book *Guns, Germs, and Steel: The Fates of Human Societies*. Diamond contends that Western Europeans came to dominate the world not because of any special intelligence or capability on their part but because of a unique geographical inheritance that gave them distinct advantages over other regions of the world. Specifically, Diamond argues that by the luck of geography, the Eurasian continent was well supplied with many wild ancestors of domesticated animals and cereal grains. Moreover, the lengthy east-west axis of Eurasia (which is also closely connected to northern Africa) facilitated the relatively easy transmission of domesticated plant and animal species across this most expansive of continents. Thus, the people of Eurasia were able to develop and share not only methods of agriculture and animal husbandry but also metallurgy, writing, gunpowder, and navigation at a rapid pace compared to other regions of the world.[4]

Diamond's model shows how Western Europe had a sort of geographical "head start" in the competition for world influence, but it does not explain everything about Western European dominance. Other cultural, political, and economic developments also enhanced both the desire and ability of Western European societies to project their power across oceans. Most important, by the 1500s and 1600s, Western Europe had developed a set of competing nation-states—a particularly potent form of political organization that fused economic, military, and religious power. England's forays across the Atlantic ocean in the late 1500s were very much connected to the competition between the emerging English

2   Helen C. Rountree, *Pocahontas, Powhatan, and Opechancanough: Three Indian Lives Changed by Jamestown* (Charlottesville: University of Virginia Press, 2006), 50.

3   Townsend, *Powhatan Dilemma*, 23–24.

4   Jared M. Diamond, *Guns, Germs, and Steel: The Fates of Human Societies* (New York: W.W. Norton, 1998).

nation-state and that of Spain, the then-dominant Atlantic power whose fabled armada the English had defeated in 1588. The English Crown licensed privateers (essentially government-approved pirates) to raid Spanish treasure ships and also chartered joint-stock corporations to plant colonies abroad. Although the Virginia Company was not funded directly by the English Crown or Parliament, its existence depended on the promises of the growing overseas economy, made possible by the emergence of England as a nation-state.

Christianity, which was central to most of the nation-states that emerged in early modern Europe, also played a prominent role in supporting colonization efforts. Attempts to establish religious unity through coercion and violence magnified the power of the emerging nation-states of both Spain and England. Their rivalry was founded on both economic interest and religious commitments, as the former was Roman Catholic and the latter consistently Protestant, following the accession of Queen Elizabeth to the English throne in 1558. In both cases, too, Christian beliefs supported overseas expeditions. Early modern Catholics and Protestants both believed they had a mandate to spread their faiths. This mandate played a significant role in justifying and mobilizing for the creation of empires in the Americas.

Given that Catholics and Protestants alike tended to view non-Christian people as "heathens" who were by definition uncivilized, religious views also shaped the process of colonization. English colonizers hoped that Native people—whom they presumed to be "savages"—would generally welcome them not only as trading partners and allies but as bearers of Christian civilization. As Robert Johnson wrote in a book promoting the Virginia settlement, published in London in 1609, the English believed that they could rescue "the poor soules" of the Native people of Virginia, "not by stormes of raging cruelties (as West India was converted) with rapiers point and musket shot, murdering so many millions of naked Indians, . . . but by faire and loving meanes, suiting to our English natures."[5]

The Powhatans did not conform to these English fantasies. Even as Chief Powhatan negotiated with the English and tried to learn more about their tools, weapons, and intentions, he also deployed allied tribes against the fledgling settlement of Jamestown and its eventual subsidiaries. The English, of course, had no way of knowing that both the apparently friendly and the openly hostile Native peoples were acting on the authority of the same leader. A modest attack on the partially completed fort at Jamestown in late May 1607 mobilized only about two hundred of Powhatan's few thousand warriors and did not destroy the settlement.

Clearly, Powhatan could have eliminated the colony entirely, but he chose not to do so. The question is, why? Based on his interactions with John Smith, whom Powhatan soon adopted as a son, and Captain Newport, who gave Powhatan gifts, the werowance probably believed that he could contain and control the English while benefiting from trade with them. In doing so, he might also prevent the English from allying with rival tribes in the region—an important consideration. In fact, Powhatan's strategy of containing the English almost worked. The harsh winter of 1609–1610, which occurred just after John Smith returned to England, left the colony so weak that Jamestown was briefly

---

5   Robert Johnson, *Nova Britannia: Offering Most Excellent Fruits by Planting in Virginia* (London, 1609; reprint New York, 1867), C2. The irregular spellings here were quite common to writings of this time. See "Note on Spelling in Primary Sources" below.

abandoned. What Powhatan did not and could not have fully appreciated, however, was the astounding ability of the English to project power across the Atlantic Ocean. Nor could he have fully understood the Virginia Company's willingness to pump seemingly endless resources into the colony to make good its members' investments. The near collapse of the colony was a result, in part, of the loss of a resupply ship in a deadly Atlantic storm. Only the arrival of supplies and reinforcements under the command of newly appointed governor, Lord De La Warr, at a critical moment, allowed for the colony's survival.[6]

Some historians have suggested that if Powhatan had decided to do so, he could have completely wiped out the Jamestown settlement during its first year, with the implication being that he made a strategic mistake by allowing the struggling settlement to survive. Indeed, Powhatan's decision to allow John Smith to live (whether Pocahontas actually intervened to save his life or not) seems to have helped the colony survive its initial two years. We might ask, then, did Powhatan make a mistake? Would he and his people have fared better if he had struck a demolishing blow against Jamestown during its first few years?

It is not possible to answer a counterfactual question such as this with certainty, but Townsend describes Powhatan's thought process as follows: "even if he could manage to defeat the current colonists by spending all his political capital and mustering every single warrior in all the tributary tribes, there would be an extraordinary number of deaths, and more English would probably come."[7] Powhatan may well have made such a calculation. In any case, he had many factors to weigh: the possibility of retribution from the English, if he did destroy their settlement; his desire for access to trade goods, including firearms that might strengthen his position against future European incursions as well as against Native rivals and enemies; and the possibility of strengthening his own position in Tsenacommacah through an alliance with the English. In short, Powhatan likely believed that he had a lot to gain from an alliance with the English—and a lot to lose if he dismissed them. Moreover, Powhatan's attempt to forge an alliance by adopting Smith was consistent with the cultural norms of his people. It made sense for him to use time-tested diplomatic and military strategies to convert the English into his tributaries, just as he had done with dozens of tribes before, and thereby to reap the benefits of trading with the English while keeping them on his side.

It is important to recognize that, even as Powhatan sought to establish an exclusive diplomatic and trade relationship with the English, he also exerted considerable effort trying to contain them. In other words, Powhatan hedged his bets—taking advantage of the fact that the English had no way of knowing the full extent of his reach. He could bargain with the English while at the same time sending his tributaries to make a restrained attack. Upon the first arrival of the English, Powhatan apparently authorized multiple strikes against them, probably to dissuade them from settling down while also testing their strength. Having the good fortune of capturing John Smith in late 1607, Powhatan adopted him, hoping to make the English his tributaries.

Soon, however, the strategic situation shifted. Over the next few years, the English became quite dependent on Powhatan for corn. They demanded more and more corn

---

6   Ian K. Steele, *Warpaths: Invasions of North America* (New York: Oxford University Press, 1994), 42–43.

7   Townsend, *Powhatan Dilemma*, 60.

at the same time that a drought seriously reduced the food supply in Tsenacommacah. No longer able to depend on Powhatan's strategically offered charity, the English aggressively sought out food. By the time that Smith departed in October 1609, the English and the Powhatans were at war. With Powhatan warriors hemming them in, many Englishmen starved, and the colony was saved from failure only by the arrival of Lord De La Warr in June of 1610.

The reinforcements and supplies brought by De La Warr strengthened the hand of the English considerably, and they launched numerous raids and attacks against the Powhatans over the next few years. Notably, Captain Samuel Argall took Pocahontas prisoner in April of 1613. While in captivity, Pocahontas received Christian instruction. A year later, she was baptized and agreed to marry Englishman John Rolfe, after consulting her father through intermediaries. Thus, the war ended; and for several years, the English and Powhatans coexisted in Tsenacommacah in relative peace.

Throughout these conflicts, the steel weapons, armor, and firearms of the English certainly gave them an advantage, but it is important not to overestimate the signifance of personal firearms in securing English victory. The Powhatans were quite skilled in the use of their traditional weapons, and English muskets were comparatively heavy, slow, and prone to malfunction. Nonetheless, the Powhatans did desire to possess guns, and this desire encouraged them to form an alliance and trade with the English. Within a dozen years or so of the founding of Jamestown, some Powhatan men had acquired and were able to use muskets—and the Powhatans' use of firearms only expanded over time. In the early conflicts between the English and Powhatans, it was the English cannons, which could be mounted on boats and trained on Powhatan villages, that likely proved more decisive in giving the English a military advantage.

With the conclusion of the First Anglo-Powhatan War, the English continued their struggle to make their colony profitable. It was John Rolfe, probably with some help from Pocahontas, who perfected the art of growing and curing tobacco and thus discovered the cash crop that allowed the colony to prosper and grow over the next several decades. The strong and growing demand for tobacco in England generated a powerful motivation for the English to put increasing swaths of the fertile Chesapeake landscape into production and to import indentured laborers to assist in the effort. By 1618, the colony implemented a "headright" system of distributing land, which offered fifty acres of land for any family members, servants, or, eventually, African slaves brought into the colony. In the half century between 1630 and 1680, about 50,000 indentured servants immigrated to Virginia. Most of them were men who were put to work growing tobacco on land recently appropriated from the Powhatans.[8]

The marriage of Rolfe and Pocahontas, and the several years of peace that followed, provided new opportunities for the Powhatans to learn more about the English, their motives, and their capabilities. In 1616, Rolfe took Pocahontas on a trip to England. This trip had distinct purposes for its different participants. Officially, the visit was intended to promote the Virginia Colony (and Rolfe's tobacco product). But Pocahontas was accompanied by several Powhatans, including the elder medicine person Uttamatomakkin (Tomocomo), who was

---

8   Brendan Wolfe and Martha McCartney, "Indentured Servants in Colonial Virginia," in *Encylopedia Virginia*. Retrieved from http://encyclopediavirginia.org/Indentured_Servants_in_Colonial_Virginia.

apparently tasked with bringing back intelligence about England to share with Powhatan. Neither Pocahontas (who became sick and died near the end of the trip) or her young son, Thomas (who remained in England with a guardian for many years), made the return trip in 1617; but Uttamatomakkin did return home, carrying disturbing news about the size of the English population that surely informed Powhatan policy over the next several years.[9]

Uttamatomakkin or other members of Pocahontas's entourage may also have been carrying pathogens from England in their bodies: an epidemic struck the Powhatans in 1617. Continued contact with the English led to another outbreak of disease in 1619. Nonetheless, the diplomatic efforts made by the Powhatans increased during this period, as Opechancanough himself facilitated the intermingling of his people with the English and permitted Christian proselytization. Meanwhile, the English continued to expand aggressively onto Powhatan lands, demonstrating the ineffectiveness of the Powhatans' diplomatic strategy.

The deaths of Powhatan and Pocahontas and the eventual emergence of Opechancanough as paramount chief provided an opportunity for the Powhatans to adopt a less conciliatory strategy. In 1622, with the Powhatan population somewhat diminished by disease and their lands under increasing threat of seizure by the English, Opechancanough launched a surprise attack that devastated the English, killing a quarter of their people in one day. Historians debate Opechancanough's strategy: did he hope to drive the English out of Tsenacommacah entirely, or was he making a forceful attempt to put the English back in their place and limit their future expansion? Whichever of these outcomes he hoped for, he achieved neither. The 1622 attack, along with the even more deadly 1644 attack, managed only to justify a terribly destructive response by the English. Neither attack deterred further English expansion for long.

It seems, then, that the Powhatans attempted a full range of responses to the arrival of the English—trying everything from diplomacy to petty violence to full-scale war—and none of these strategies managed to thwart English expansion or even to slow it down for very long. In the earliest years of the colony, Powhatan perhaps had the ability to eradicate the colony, but he had little reason to do so. Once the English had established the colony's profitability, however, Native efforts at diplomatic resistance were ineffective, and their violent resistance was largely counterproductive. The pursuit of profit gave the English a powerful motive to expand the colony at the expense of the Powhatans; their belief in their own superiority provided a justification; and the emerging English nation-state (with its unprecedented ability to project power across a vast ocean) provided the means. In the sober words of Camilla Townsend, "White settlers wanted the Indians' land and had the strength to take it."[10] They would do so not only in seventeenth-century Virginia but across North America over the next two centuries. The Powhatan defeat, then, was less the result of strategic mistakes on the part of their leadership than of the daunting power imbalance between the Powhatans and the English colonizers. Ultimately, the Native survivors of this conflict would have to rely on diplomacy and their own resilience, rather than on warfare, to preserve what they could of their sovereignty and cultural heritage in the absence of the land base that had sustained their nations since time out of mind.

---

9   Townsend, *Powhatan Dilemma*, 135–158.
10   Townsend, *Powhatan Dilemma*, 178.

POSITION #2—STRATEGIC MISTAKES OF THE POWHATANS

Many historians see Werowance Powhatan along with his war chief and successor Opechancanough as shrewd strategists who were simply overwhelmed by the English colonizers—with their deadly diseases, metal armor and firearms, and bottomless appetite for land. Although it is true that Powhatan had assembled an impressive chiefdom in Tsenacommacah during the late 1500s and early 1600s, he and Opechancanough made mistakes in their dealings with the English—mistakes that cost them control over their homelands. Had he acted more decisively, Powhatan could probably have eliminated the Jamestown settlement during its early years before the English discovered and mastered the art of producing highly demanded Spanish tobacco (as opposed to the variety of tobacco grown by Native people of mainland North America). Without this clear path to profit, the struggling Virginia Company of London may well have given up, much as the Virginia Company of Plymouth folded after the failure of its colony (several hundred miles to the north) in late 1607 and early 1608. To say that the Virginia Company of London might have failed is not to say that Tsenacommacah, which offered very fertile and water-accessible land, would never have been colonized by Europeans. But the story could have turned out quite differently than it did.

Powhatan had the strategic intelligence that he needed to justify the eradication of the Jamestown colony, and he was not innocent of warfare, as indicated not only by his use of force to assemble his chiefdom but also his documented assaults on both the English and also the Chesapeake tribe. He surely knew about the experiences of Paquiquineo (also known by the Spanish name Don Luis de Velasco), the Tsenacommacah native who was kidnapped and taken to Spain and Mexico and who colluded in the destruction of the Spanish mission established in his homeland in 1571. Although the destruction of the mission provoked retribution, the Spanish opted not to attempt another settlement in the Chesapeake. Perhaps, Powhatan may have wondered, the English could have been likewise persuaded to focus their energies elsewhere? Powhatan also knew something about the Roanoke settlement of the English, which had been abandoned after two failed attempts—the most recent of which had concluded just seventeen years earlier. Powhatan did not have any way to understand in detail the origins and motivations of these wayfarers, but he was aware of these two clear precedents of failed settlements.

The 104 Englishmen who founded Jamestown in the spring of 1607 hardly qualified as an existential threat to Powhatan's chiefdom and its approximately 15,000 inhabitants. Powhatan could have ordered the destruction of the Jamestown fort, or more likely, he could have ensured the starvation of the ill-provisioned strangers. Given what happened subsequently, it is hard to believe that Powhatan spared the English out of a sense of mercy or compassion, although contemporary Powhatan Mattaponi authors Linwood "Little Bear" Custalow and Angela L. Daniel "Little Star" have argued just that. (The Mattaponi tribe belonged to the Powhatan alliance at the time of English arrival to Tsenacommacah.) Powhatan was essentially a warlord with a few thousand warriors at his disposal. He might have seen to the rapid failure of Jamestown if he had decided on that as a strategy for persuading the English to move along.[11]

It seems, however, that Chief Powhatan underestimated the threat posed by the English. He decided to try to learn more about them and to benefit from exchange with them, hoping that he could remain in control. Although the Powhatans initially tried to discourage the English from putting down roots in Tsenacommacah, in December of 1607 and January of 1608, Powhatan made the mistake of allowing his captive John Smith to return to Jamestown, having sealed a tentative alliance. Much later, in 1624, Smith told his famous story of how Powhatan's daughter Pocahontas had intervened to prevent him from being executed. Although most present-day historians question the accuracy of Smith's account, subsequent events bear out the idea that Smith was adopted by Powhatan. As Smith explained in his *General Historie of Virginia*, following the ordeal of his captivity, Powhatan "told him now they were friends, and presently he should go to Jamestown, to send him two great guns, and a grindstone, for which he would give him the county of Capahowosick, and for ever esteem him as his son Nantaquoud."[12]

Powhatan did indeed offer some assistance to the English over the next year, helping ensure their survival. Meanwhile, the English neglected to take measures to provide food for themselves. By late 1608, it became clear to the Powhatans that they did not have enough food for both themselves and the English. Drought had taken a toll on corn yields, and the Powhatans could no longer accede to English demands. The English could not take "no" for an answer: they used force to take what they needed to survive. Thus the initial alliance that Powhatan had tried to forge by adopting Smith came to an end, after less than one year.[13] According to Smith's 1624 account, Powhatan at this time made a plea for peaceful coexistence. But the English were sufficiently desperate for provisions that Smith soon held the war chief Opechancanough at gunpoint to secure corn to feed his fellow adventurers.[14]

Powhatan's response to this English stratagem of stealing his people's food was twofold. First, he relocated his headquarters from Werowocomoco upstream to Orapax, to improve his security by making it impossible for the English to reach him in their boats. Second, he continued to withhold corn from the English, apparently hoping that they

11 Linwood "Little Bear" Custalow and Angela L. Daniel "Little Star," "The Colony Saved by the Powhatan," from *The True Story of Pocahontas: The Other Side of History* (Golden, CO: Fulcrum Publishing, 2007), 71–77.

12 John Smith, *The Generall Historie of Virginia, New England & the Summer Isles, Together with the True Travels, Adventures and Observations, and A Sea Grammar*, Vol. 1: Ch. II. 1624; Reprint New York: Macmillan, 1907. From the Library of Congress, at http://memory.loc.gov/cgi-bin/query/h?ammem/lhbcbbib:@field(NUMBER+@band(lhbcb+0262a))

13 Helen C. Rountree, *Pocahontas, Powhatan, and Opechancanough: Three Indian Lives Changed by Jamestown* (Charlottesville: University of Virginia Press, 2006), 119–120.

14 Rountree, *Pocahontas, Powhatan, and Opechancanough*, 120–121, 125–127.

would starve—and many did. As Helen Rountree has argued, "Powhatan and his people played a major role in the 'Starving Time' that the denizens of Jamestown endured in the winter of 1609–10," shortly after Smith returned to England after being injured in an accidental gunpowder explosion.[15]

During this winter, the English population dwindled from 240 to about 60. Meanwhile, back in England, the financial support for the colony was languishing. By 1612, the Virginia Company of London would resort to a dubious lottery to raise funds.[16] Investors might soon have decided to cut their losses. If Powhatan had struck a decisive blow against the English in 1610, he might have ended the project then and there. But he missed this moment of opportunity, giving the beleaguered English a chance to recover.[17]

As of 1610, Powhatan still held the upper hand, in terms of his ability to mobilize warriors and to control the food supply in Tsenacommacah; yet after several years of ongoing warfare, he decided to accept English overtures for peace by authorizing the marriage of his daughter Pocahontas to John Rolfe in 1614.[18] A relatively peaceful interlude of eight years gave the English time to develop tobacco as a steady source of profit, which stabilized the colony, drew hundreds of new settlers, and gave the English strong incentives for stealing Powhatan land. The several years after the 1614 truce, in other words, marked a critical turning point for the Virginia Colony. By 1622, even the large-scale surprise assault on the English settlements, directed by Opechancanough, failed to either contain or destroy the colony. The tide had turned, and it turned because Powhatan pursued coexistence rather than continuing to fight against the colony while it remained vulnerable. Historian J. Frederick Fausz has argued that the Powhatans "relied too much on their traditional military prowess to protect their culture from outside influences," and their overconfidence ultimately enabled the English to dispossess them.[19]

Unbeknownst to Powhatan, his daughter's suitor, Rolfe, held the future of the colony in his hands. The colony had yet to turn a profit, and it was becoming increasingly difficult to fund the project. Rolfe had been experimenting with the growing of so-called Spanish tobacco, which had actually been domesticated by indigenous people in South America and appropriated by the Spanish as a commodity. Rolfe's initial tobacco crop, shipped to England in 1613, was deemed adequate but still inferior to tobacco grown and cured in the Spanish colonies, using proprietary methods.

Although seventeenth-century records are silent about the role that his marriage to Pocahontas played in the success of his tobacco-growing experiments, it is probably no coincidence that the tobacco Rolfe produced in the first full season after his marriage

15 Rountree, *Pocahontas, Powhatan, and Opechancanough,* 129, 134.

16 Brendan Wolfe, "Virginia Company of London," in *Encyclopedia Virginia.* Retrieved from http://www.encyclopediavirginia.org/Virginia_Company_of_London.

17 Brendan Wolfe argues that the winter of 1609–1610 was "Powhatan's best chance to win the war and to evict the English colonists from Tsenacomoco," and he neglected to take advantage of it. See "First Anglo-Powhatan War (1609–1614)" in *Encyclopedia Virginia.* Retrieved from http://www.EncyclopediaVirginia.org/First_Anglo-Powhatan_War_1609-1614.

18 Camilla Townsend, *Pocahontas and the Powhatan Dilemma* (New York: Hill & Wang, 2005), 124–134.

19 J. Frederick Fausz, "The Invasion of Virginia: Indians, Colonialism, and the Conquest of Cant: A Review Essay on Anglo-Indian Relations in the Chesapeake," *Virginia Magazine of History and Biography* 95 (April 1987), 133–156; see 145.

to Pocahontas had improved sufficiently in quality over previous shipments that it was judged to be competitive with the Spanish product. Indeed, according to Linwood "Little Bear" Custalow and Angela L. Daniel "Little Star," the Powhatan Mattaponi oral tradition conveys that Rolfe used his relationship with Pocahontas to obtain secret knowledge from the Powhatan *quiakros* (or "priests," in English parlance) about how to cure the tobacco to produce an appealingly flavored product. In the words of Custalow and Daniel: "The Powhatan actually saved the colony by sharing their knowledge of tobacco curing and management. This sharing of knowledge was directly linked to Wahunsenaca and his daughter Pocahontas . . . because he wanted to be friends, at peace, in alliance with the English from the beginning."[20] The historical record is ambiguous regarding Powhatan's desire for friendship "from the beginning," but this claim otherwise rings true. Kinship ties were of central importance in Powhatan society, and it makes sense that Rolfe could have utilized his new connections to learn what he needed to know to perfect his ability to cure tobacco. Having permitted the marriage of his daughter to his recent opponents, Powhatan seemed substantially committed to making peace with the English. Why not offer this kind of material assistance, as he had done in the past when he adopted Smith and helped feed the English?

The results of the successful cultivation of tobacco were, of course, disastrous for the Powhatan people. As Custalow and Daniel note, "Instead of the English colonists embracing the Powhatan people and becoming their allies, the colonists' greed was unleashed."[21] Once Rolfe had successfully produced a marketable tobacco crop, the plant became the very heart of a new economy that would draw tens of thousands of English settlers to the Chesapeake over the next several decades—settlers with an insatiable hunger for land. Tobacco thus saved the Virginia Colony but led to the massive dispossession of the Powhatan people.

As early as 1608–1609, when the settlers first began to seize Native food supplies by force, Powhatan had reasons to know that English were not to be trusted. And yet, rather than take decisive steps against the invaders, Powhatan repeatedly sought to find a way to coexist with the Virginia colonists. By the time Powhatan's successor Opechancanough recognized the magnitude of the threat and launched the 1622 assault, it was too late. The Virginia Colony was too well established, and the English crown's commitment to its success too deep, for the colony to be removed by force. The Powhatans lost their opportunity to eject the English while they still could.

---

20 Custalow and Daniel, *True Story of Pocahontas*, 76.
21 Ibid.

DEBATING THE QUESTION

INTRODUCTION

The primary sources that follow were each created by a particular person (or group) for specific reasons. Each source comes from a perspective and must be treated with care. No source can be taken purely at face value. Each source must be interpreted in light of the author and the author's motives.

It is especially important to recognize that the English had a monopoly on the creation of written documents about the Chesapeake during this period. Powhatan voices come to us only indirectly through English documents, though some tribal oral traditions have been preserved and passed down to the present. (See the source by Linwood "Little Bear" Custalow and Angela L. Daniel "Little Star," "The Colony Saved by the Powhatan.") The English written documents might initially seem more reliable than the Native oral tradition, simply because they were fixed in writing much closer to the time that the events took place. In some cases, this bias of historians in favor of written documentation may serve us well, but in other cases, less so. For example, the three sources provided here that were created by John Smith are all of questionable accuracy and legitimacy. Smith's account of being rescued by Pocahontas in 1607 has been challenged by historians and the Mattaponi oral tradition alike. (The Mattaponi tribe was part of the Powhatan alliance. See the reading titled "Accounts of John Smith's December 1607 Captivity" in the section "Case Study 1.") His account of a 1608 "Speech of Powhatan" may ring more true, but its accuracy is also questionable given he did not publish the account until 1624. Likewise, the authenticity of his alleged 1616 letter to Queen Anne about Pocahontas is highly uncertain. (See the reading titled "John Smith's Alleged 1616 Letter to Queen Anne regarding Pocahontas" in the section "Case Study 1.")

The problem is not simply that sources can be fabricated or embroidered: all sources embed a point of view. In the case of the conflict between the English and Powhatans, the two groups had very different ways of understanding the world, which means that they often misunderstood each other. See, for example, "Captain Christopher Newport's Description of Virginia (1607)" in the "Primary Sources" section, in which he makes assumptions and judgments about the Native inhabitants of the Chesapeake region. To what extent are his observations and evaluations to be trusted?

Whether the sources are written, oral, visual, or artifactual, historians are left to scrutinize them carefully and to analyze them within the context of all the other available primary sources.

The source materials also include two case studies that contain a selection of both scholarly writings and additional primary sources focused on particular issues: namely, the alleged 1607 rescue of John Smith by Pocahontas and the 1622 Powhatan surprise attack against the English, orchestrated by Opechancanough.

NOTE ON LANGUAGE AND SPELLING IN PRIMARY SOURCES

The historical essays above (and the editorial headnotes below) refer to specific tribal nations by name when possible (Powhatan, Pamunkey, Mattaponi, and so on). When a more general label is needed, they usually refer to "Native people," "Native peoples" (to indicate a variety of tribal nations), or, especially in a present-day context, "Native Americans." This approach avoids the disrespectful practice of lumping together diverse indigenous groups.

During the historical period under scrutiny, however, the English frequently referred to Native people as "savages" (with various spellings, including "salvages") and collectively as "the Indians." Although the English certainly recognized differences among the many tribal nations and cultures that they encountered in North America, they frequently threw aside such distinctions, especially during times of conflict.

With careful use of language, instructors and students can avoid reinforcing the ethnocentric views of the seventeenth-century English colonizers that are on full display in the primary documents below. For many historical questions in this book, the most salient labels for the Native people in question will be "the Powhatans" or "the Powhatan people" (rather than "the Indians" or "the Natives").

The historical documents included here date to the late sixteenth century or seventeenth century. For some documents, the spellings have been modernized throughout, or clarification provided in brackets; but in other documents, the spelling is true to the original to reflect the style of the time.

In some cases, the letter "u" is rendered as a "v." Thus "vs" means "us" and "haue" means "have," and so forth. Additionally, an "i" is sometimes used instead of the "y" in modern English; thus "eies" means "eyes" and "waies" means "ways." Sometimes, the opposite situation applies, and a "y" is used where an "i" would appear in modern English. Occasionally, an "i" appears where modern spellings use a "j," as in "subiection" for "subjection." Double consonants are used less regularly than in modern English. Some documents use "att" instead of "at" and "unles" instead of "unless," for example. In many cases, if you are having trouble deciphering a word, if you try to pronounce the word phonetically you will recognize the modern equivalent. For example, the initially puzzling "connynge" reveals itself as "cunning" when pronounced.

PRIMARY SOURCES

1.1 RICHARD HAKLUYT (THE YOUNGER), *DISCOURSE ON WESTERN PLANTING* (1584)

Richard Hakluyt (the Younger), along with his cousin of the same name, was a highly influential promotor of the English colonization of the North American mainland. The following excerpt from his 1584 *Discourse on Western Planting* summarizes the key points of his comprehensive argument in favor of colonization projects. Note that Hakluyt uses the name "Norumbega," a legendary settlement, to refer to eastern North America.

GUIDING QUESTIONS:

1. What various incentives did Hakluyt identify for English colonization of North America?
2. What are Hakluyt's assumptions about the Native inhabitants, whom he calls "naturall people," of North America? What are his motives with regard to them?

A BRIEFE COLLECTION OF CERTAINE REASONS TO INDUCE HER MAJESTIE AND THE STATE TO TAKE IN HANDE THE WESTERNE VOYADGE AND THE PLANTINGE THERE

1. The soyle yeldeth, and may be made to yelde, all the severall comodities of Europe, and of all kingdomes, domynions, and territories that England tradeth withe, that by trade of marchandize cometh into this realme. . . .

6. This enterprise may staye the Spanishe Kinge from flowinge over all the face of that waste firme of America. . . . And England possessinge the purposed place of plantinge, her Majestie may, by the benefete of the seate, havinge wonne goodd and royall havens, have plentie of excellent trees for mastes, of goodly timber to builde shippes and to make great navies, of pitche, tarr, hempe, and all thinges incident for a navie royall, and that for no price, and withoute money or request. Howe easie a matter may yt be to this realme, swarminge at this day with valiant youthes, rustinge and hurtfull by lacke of employment, and havinge goodd makers of cable and of all sortes of cordage, and the best and moste connynge shipwrights of the worlde, to be lordes of all those sees, and to spoile Phillipps Indian navye, and to deprive him of yerely passage of his treasure into Europe, and consequently to abate the pride of Spaine and of the supporter of the great Antechriste of Rome, and to pull him downe in equalitie to his neighbour princes, and consequently to cut of the common mischefes that come to all Europe by the peculiar aboundance of his Indian treasure, and thiss withoute difficultie. . . .

8. This newe navie of mightie newe strong shippes, so in trade to that Norumbega and to the coastes there, shall never be subjecte to arreste of any prince or potentate, as the navie of this realme from time to time hath bene in the portes of the empire. . . .

10. No forren commoditie that comes into England comes withoute payment of custome once, twise, or thrise, before it come into the realme, and so all forren comodities become derer to the subjectes of this realme; and by this course to Norumbega forren princes customes are avoided;

Source: Richard Hakluyt, "Discourse on Western Planting," in *Documentary History of the State of Maine*, Vol. II, edited by Charles Deane (Cambridge, 1877), 152–161.

and the forren comodities cheapely purchased, they become cheape to the subjectes of England, to the common benefite of the people, and to the savinge of greate treasure in the realme; whereas nowe the realme become the poore by the purchasinge of forreine comodities in so greate a masse at so excessive prices.

11. At the firste traficque with the people of those partes, the subjectes of the realme for many yeres shall chaunge many cheape comodities of these partes for thinges of highe valor there not estemed; and this to the greate inrichinge of the realme, if common use faile not. . . .

13. By makinge of shippes and by preparinge of thinges for the same, by makinge of cables and cordage, by plantinge of vines and olive trees, and by makinge of wyne and oyle, by husbandrie, and by thousandes of thinges there to be don, infinite nombers of the English nation may be set on worke, to the unburdenynge of the realme with many that nowe lyve chardgeable to the state at home.

14. If the sea coste serve for makinge of salte, and the inland for wine, oiles, oranges, lymons, figges, &c. and for makinge of yron, all which with moche more is hoped, withoute sworde drawen, wee shall cutt the combe of the Frenche, of the Spanishe, of the Portingale, and of enemies, and of doubtfull frendes, to the abatinge of their wealthe and force, and to the greater savinge of the wealthe of the realme.

15. The substaunces servinge, wee may oute of those partes receave the masse of wrought wares that now wee receave out of Fraunce, Flaunders, Germanye, &c.: and so wee may daunte the pride of some enemies of this realme, or at the leaste in parte purchase those wares, that nowe wee buye derely of the Frenche and Flemynge, better cheape; and in the ende, for the part that this realme was wonte to receave, dryve them out of trade to idlenes for the setting of our people on worke.

16. Wee shall by plantinge there inlarge the glory of the gospell, and from England plante sincere religion, and provide a safe and a sure place to receave people from all partes of the worlde that are forced to flee for the truthe of Gods worde.

17. If frontier warres there chaunce to aryse, and if thereupon wee shall fortifie, yt will occasion the trayninge upp of our youthe in the discipline of warr, and make a nomber fitt for the service of the warres and for the defence of our people there and at home.

18. The Spaniardes governe in the Indies with all pride and tyranie; and like as when people of contrarie nature at the sea enter into gallies, where men are tied as slaves, all yell and crye with one voice, *Liberta, liberta*, as desirous of libertie and freedome, so no doubte whensoever the Queene of England, a prince of such clemencie, shall seate upon that firme of America, and shalbe reported throughe oute all that tracte to use the naturall people there with all humanitie, curtesie, and freedome, they will yelde themselves to her governemente, and revolte cleane from the Spaniarde, and specially when they shall understande that she hath a noble navie, and that she aboundeth with a people moste valiaunte for theyr defence. . . .

20. Many men of excellent wittes and of divers singuler giftes, overthrowen by sea, or by some folly of youthe, that are not able to live in England, may there be raised againe, and doe their contrie goodd service; and many nedefull uses there may (to greate purpose) require the savinge of greate nombers, that for trifles may otherwise be devoured by the gallowes.

21. Many souldiers and servitours, in the ende of the warres, that mighte be hurtfull to this realme, may there be unladen, to the common profite and quiet of this realme, and to our forreine benefite there, as they may be employed.

22. The frye of the wandringe beggars of England, that growe upp ydly, and hurtefull and burdenous to this realme, may there be unladen, better bredd upp, and may people waste contries to the home and forreine benefite, and to their owne more happy state.

DRAWING CONCLUSIONS:

1. How did Hakluyt make the case that the colonization of North America was important to English interests?

2. Given these motivations and incentives, how were the English likely to perceive and treat the Native people they would encounter in North America?

1.2   ARTISTIC DEPICTION OF A NATIVE VILLAGE SOUTH OF THE CHESAPEAKE BAY (1590)

The following image was printed in a 1590 edition of Thomas Hariot's book, *A Briefe and True Report of the New Found Land of Virginia*, which was first published in London in 1588. The book's many engravings by Theodor de Bry were based on original watercolor paintings made by John White. Both Hariot and White had been at the "lost" Roanoke colony in 1585–1586 but departed before the colony's collapse. In addition to spending time on Roanoke Island, they visited the mainland (modern-day North Carolina). Although Hariot's descriptions and White's depictions came from the region just south of the Chesapeake Bay, they nonetheless served as an important source of information for the Virginia Company as it planned its settlement.

GUIDING QUESTION:

1.   How did this image and description from Hariot's book depict the Native inhabitants whom the English would expect to encounter as they colonized eastern North America?

"THE NATIVE AMERICAN VILLAGE OF SECOTA"

DRAWING CONCLUSIONS:

1.   What expectations might this depiction and description of a Native American village have created for the founders of the Jamestown colony?

2.   What can we learn about the Native cultures of the Chesapeake region from this depiction?

FIGURE 1. JOHN WHITE, "THE NATIVE AMERICAN VILLAGE OF SECOTA" (1590).
Thomas Hariot's caption:
The Tovvne of Secota. Their townes that are not inclosed with poles aire commonlye fayrer. Then suche as are inclosed, as appereth in this figure which liuelye expresseth the towne of Secotam. For the howses are Scattered heer and ther, and they haue gardein expressed by the letter E. wherin groweth Tobacco which the inhabitants call Vppowoc. They haue also groaues wherin thei take deer, and fields vherin they sowe their corne. In their corne fields they builde as yt weare a scaffolde wher on they sett a cottage like to a rownde chaire, signiffied by F. wherin they place one to watche for there are suche number of fowles, and beasts, that vnless they keepe the better watche, they would soone deuoure all their corne. For which cause the watcheman maketh continual cryes and noyse. They sowe their corne with a certaine distance noted by H. otherwise one stalke would choke the growthe of another and the corne would not come vnto his rypeurs G. For the leaues therof are large, like vnto the leaues of great reedes. They haue also a seuerall broade plotte C. whear they meete with their neighbours, to celebrate their cheefe solemne feastes . . . and a place D. whear after they haue ended their feaste they make merrie togither. Ouer against this place they haue a rownd plott B. wher they assemble themselues to make their solemne prayers. Not far from which place ther is a lardge buildinge A. wherin are the tombes of their kings and princes, . . . likewise they haue [a] garden notted bey the letter I. wherin they vse to sowe pompions. Also a place marked with K. wherin the make a fyre att their solemne feasts, and hard without the towne a riuer L. from whence they fetche their water. This people therfore voyde of all couetousnes lyue cherfullye and att their harts ease. Butt they solemnise their feasts in the nigt, and therfore they keepe verye great fyres to auoyde darkenes, ant to testifie their loye.
Source: The Village of Secoton, from 'Admiranda Narratio . . .', published by Theodore de Bry (coloured engraving), Bry, Theodore de (1528–98), after White, John (d.1593) / Service Historique de la Marine, Vincennes, France / Bridgeman Images

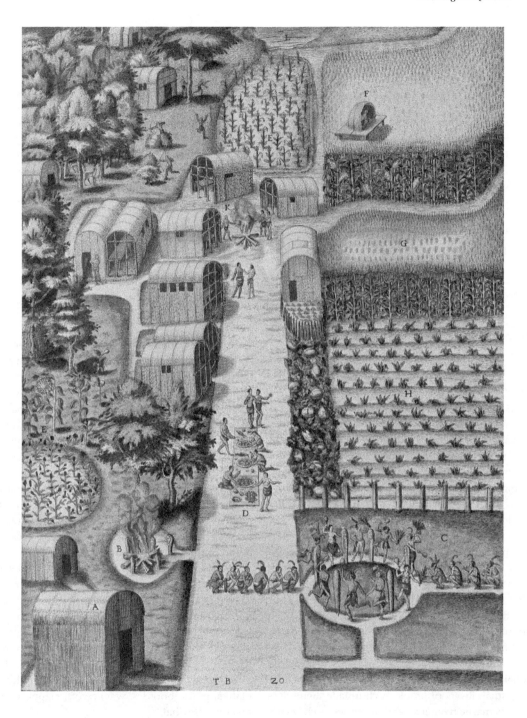

1.3 CAPTAIN CHRISTOPHER NEWPORT'S DESCRIPTION OF VIRGINIA (1607)

Captain Christopher Newport played an important role in establishing the Virginia Colony, including commanding the first voyage to establish the colony in 1607. In the following account from June 1607, Newport described both the land and people he saw during his initial exploration of the newly dubbed "James River." As elsewhere in the primary documents from this time, the word "salvage" is equivalent to the modern "savage," and it reflects the beliefs of the English that the Native people were not part of civilized society.

GUIDING QUESTION:

1. How did Newport describe the land and people he encountered on his excursion? What was the focus of his description?

THE DESCRIPTION OF THE NOW-DISCOVERED RIVER AND COUNTRY OF VIRGINIA, WITH THE LIKLYHOOD OF ENSUING RITCHES, BY ENGLAND'S AYD AND INDUSTRY

This river we have named o'r [our] King's river extends it self 160 myles into the Mayne land between two fertile and fragrant banks, two miles, a mile, and where it is least a quarter of a myle broad, navigable for shipping of 300 tunn 150 miles; the rest deep enough for small vessells of six foot drought; it ebbs and flowes 4 foote, even to the skirt of an overfall, where the water falls down from huge great Rocks; making in the fall five or six severall Isletts, very fitt for the buylding of water milnes thereon, beyond this not two dayes journey, it hath two branches w'ch [which] come through a high stoney countrey from certain huge mountaines called Quirank, beyond w'ch needs no relac'on (this from the overfall was the report and description of a faithful fellow, who I dare well trust upon good reasons) from these mountaines Quirank came two lesse rivers w'ch runn into this great one, but whether deep enough for shipps or noe I yet understand not, there be many small Rivers of brooks w'ch unlade themselves into this mayne river at severall mouthes, w'ch veynes divide the salvage Kingdoms in many places, and yeeld pleasant seates, in all the country over by moystering

the frutefull mould. The mayne river abounds w'th sturgeon very large and excellent good; having also at the mouth of every brook and in every creek both store and exceeding good fish of divers kinds, in ye large sounds neere the sea are multitudes of fish, banks of oysters, and many great crabbs rather better, in fact, than oures, are able to suffice 4 men, and within sight of land into the sea we expect at tyme of yeare to have a good fishing for codd, as both at o'r ent'ring [our entering] we might p'ceiv'e [perceive] by palpable conjecture seeing the codd follow the shipp yea bite at the [blank in the manuscript] as also out of my ouwne experience not farre of to the northward, the fishing I found in my first voyage to Virginia.

This land lyeth low at the mouth of the river & is sandy ground, all over besett with fayre pyne trees, but a little up the river it is reasonable high, and the further we go (till we came to the overfall) it still ryseth increasing. It is generally replenish't w'th wood of all kinds and that the fayrest yea and the best that any of us (traveller or workman) ever sawe, being fitt for use whatsoever, as shipps, howses, planks, poles, boordes, waynescott, clappboard, for pikes or elsewhat.

The soyle is more fertill than can be well exprest it is altogether aromaticall giving a spicy taste to the rootes of all trees plants and hearbs: of it self a black fatt sand mould somewhat slymy in touch and sweet in savor: under w'ch about a yard is in most places a redd clay fitt for brick, in other marle, in some signification of mynerall, in other gravell stones and rocks, it hath in diverse places fullers earth, and such as comes out of Turky called terra siggillata. It p'duceth [produces] of one come [corne?] of that country wheate some-times two or three stems or stalks on w'ch grow eares above a spann long besett w'th comes at least, 300 upon an eare for the most part 5, 6 & 700. the beanes and peaz of this country have a great increase also: It yeelds two cropps a yeare. Being temp(er)ed and tyme taken I hold it natures nurse to all vigitables for I assure myself no knoune continent brings forth any vendible necessaryes w'h this by planting will not afford: for testimony in part, this we fynd by proof: from the west Indies we brought a certaine delicious fruite called a pina, w'ch the Spanyard by all art possible could never p'cure to grow in any place, but in his natural site, this we rudely and carelessly sett in o'r mould, w'ch fostereth it and keeps it greene. and to what Issue it may come I know not, our west Indy plants of orenges & cotton trees thrive well, likewise the potatoes, pumpious & millions: All o'r garden seeds, that were carefully soune p[ro]sper well, yet we only digged the ground half a [missing word] deep throw in the seeds at randome carelessly, and scarce rakt it. It naturally yeelds mulbery trees, cherry trees, vines aboundance, gooseberryes, strawberryes, huckleberryes, Respesses, ground nutts, scarretts, the roote called sigilla christi, certain sweet thym, shelled nutts, certaine ground aples, a pleasant fruite any [missing word] Many other unknown. So the thing we crave is some skillful man to husband, sett, plant, and dresse vynes, sugar canes, olives ropes hemp flax, lyceris pruynes, currants, raysons, and all such things, as the north Tropick of the world offords: also saffran woad hoppes and such like.

The comodityes of the country, what they are in else, is not much to be regarded, the inhabitants having no concerne w'h any nation, no respect of p[ro]fitt, neither is there scarce that we call *meum et tuum* [mine and yours, i.e., private property], among them save onely the Kings know their owne territoryes, & the people their severall gardens yet this for the present by the consent of all o'r seamen, meerly o'r fyshing for sturgeon, cannot be lesse worth then 1,000 £ [pounds] a yeare, leaving hering and codd as possibilitys.

Our clapboard and waynscott (if shipps will but fetch it) we may make as much as England can vent: We can send (if we be frends w'h the salvage or be able to force them) 2, 3, 4, or 5,000 £ a yeare of the earth called *terra siggillala*. Saxafroge what store we pleast. Tobacco after a yeare or two 5,000 £ a year. We have (as we suppose) ritch dyes, if they p[ro]ve vendible, worth more than yet is nominated; We have excellant furrs, in some places of the country great store; we can make pitch Rozen and Turpentyne; there is a gume w'ch bleedeth from a kind of maple (the bark being cutt) not much unlike a Balsome both in sent and vertue. Hepothicary druggs of diverse sorts, some known to be of good estimacon, some strange of whose vertue the salvages report wonders—We can by o'r industry and plantacon of comodious marchandisze make oyles wynes soape ashes, wood ashes, extract from minerall earth Iron copper etc.; We have a good fishing for musles, w'ch resemble mother of pearle, & if the pearle we have seene in the Kings eares & about their necks come from these shells we know the banks. To conclude I know not what can be expected from a comon wealth that either this land affords not or may soone yeeld.

A BRIEF DESCRIPTION OF THE PEOPLE

There is a King in this land called great Powhatan, under whose dominion are at least 20ty severall kingdoms, yet each King potent as a prince in his own territory. These have their subjects at so quick command, as a beck brings obedience, even to the restitucon of stolen goods w'ch by their naturall inclinacon they are loth to leave. They goe almost naked, yet in coole weather they weare deare skinns, w'th the hay re on loose; some have leather stockings up to their thighs & sandalls on their feet, their hayre is black generally, w'ch they weare long on their left side, tyed up on a knott about w'ch knott the kings and best among them have a kind of coronett of deares hayre colored redd, some have chaines of long lincks copper about their necks, and some chaines of pearle, the common sort stick long fethers in this knott, I found not a gray eye among them all. Their skynn is tawny not so borne, but w'ch dying and paynting themselves, in w'ch they delight greatly. The women are like the men—only this difference their hayre groweth long al over their heads save dipt somewhat short afore, these do all the labo'r and the men hunt and goe at their pleasure. They live comonly by the water side in little cottages made of canes and reeds, covered w'th the barks of trees; they dwell as I guesse by families of kindred & allyance some 40tie or sotie in a Hatto or small village; w'ch townes are not past a myle or half a myle asunder in most places. They live upon sodden wheat beanes & peaze for the most part, also they kill deare take fish in their weares & kill fowle abundance, they eat often and that liberally; they are prop[er] lusty streight men very strong runn exceeding swiftly, their feight [fight] is alway in the wood with bow & arrowes & a short wooden sword, the celerity they use in skirmish is admirable. The King directs the battle and is alway's in front.

Their manner of entertainement is upon mattes on the ground under some tree, where they sit themselves alone in the midest of the matt, and two matts on each side, on w'ch they [re] people sitt, then right against him (making a square forme) satt we always. When they came to their matt they have another goes before them and the rest as he sitts downe give a long showt. The people steale anything comes neare them, yea are so practized in this art that looking in o'r face they would w'th their foot between their toes convey a chizell knife, peices of any indifferent light: w'ch having once conveyed they hold it an injury to take the same

from them. They are naturally given to trechery, howbeit we could not finde it in o'r travell up the river, but rather a most kind and loving people. The sacrifice Tobacco to the Sunn fayre picture or a harmeful thing, as a sword or peece also, they sprincle some into the water in the morning before they wash, they have many wives, to whome as neare as I could p'rceive they Keep constant, the great King Powhatan had most wives. . . . The women are very cleanly in making their bread and preparing meat. I found they account alter death to goe into another world pointing eastward & the element & when they saw us at prayer they observed us w'th great silence and respect, especially those to whome I had imparted the meaning of o'r reverence. To conclude they are very witty and ingenius people, apt both to understand and speake o'r language, so that I hope in God as he hath miraculously p'rserved us hither from all danger both of sea and land & their fury so he will make us authors of his holy will in converting them to o'r true christian faith by his owne inspiring grace and knowledge of his duty.

[Endorsed] Capten Newport of Virginias Discovery Virginia 21 June, 1607.

DRAWING CONCLUSIONS:

1. What assumptions about the land and people of Tsenacommacah emerge from Newport's description? How accurate were these assumptions?
2. What does this document suggest about the prospects for establishing a profitable colony in the midst of the Powhatan empire?

1.4 POWHATAN'S MANTLE (C. 1600)

Although this cloak's origins are uncertain, it was cataloged at the Ashmolean Museum (Oxford, England) in the mid-1600s and probably belonged to Chief Powhatan. Written sources record that Powhatan gifted his "mantle" to Captain Christopher Newport in 1608. Consisting of four deerskins stitched together, this mantle is 7'8" tall and 5'3" wide. The designs are made of polished sea shells. If the mantle did indeed belong to Powhatan, the circular shapes likely represent the thirty-odd tribes in his chiefdom.

GUIDING QUESTION:

1. What might this mantle have meant to Powhatan and his people?

FIGURE 2. "POWHATAN'S MANTLE" (C. 1600). *Source:* AN1685 B.205 Powhatan's Mantle, said to have been owned by Chief Wahunsunacock (died 1618), Southern Chesapeake Bay region, Virginia, United States of America, c. 1600–38, Leather, shell and sinew Image © Ashmolean Museum, University of Oxford

DRAWING CONCLUSIONS:

1. Why might Powhatan have gifted the mantle to Captain Newport?

1.5 SPEECH OF POWHATAN (1608), AS REPORTED BY JOHN SMITH (1624)

John Smith reported this speech of Powhatan in his 1624 *General History of Virginia*, about fifteen years after the event in question took place. According to Smith's account, Powhatan gave this speech during a tense (and somewhat confused) negotiation over trade and weaponry. While Powhatan demanded that the Englishmen lay down their weapons when visiting him and his people and furthermore requested swords and guns in trade, the English (represented by Smith) sought the corn they needed to survive the winter. Smith characterized Powhatan as a "subtill savage" and this speech itself as "subtill," meaning clever or cunning. The stakes for both parties at this moment were indeed high. Although the English did get some of the corn they needed in exchange for a copper kettle, they continued to resist trading firearms and other weapons for some time.

GUIDING QUESTION:

1. What sort of relationship between the English and the Powhatans does Werewance Powhatan promote in this speech attributed to him by Smith?

Captaine Smith, you may understand that I having seene the death of all my people thrice, and not any one living of these three generations but my selfe; I know the difference of Peace and Warre better then any in my Country. But now I am old and ere long must die, my brethren, namely Opitchapam, Opechanca-nough, and Kekataugh, my two sisters, and their two daughters, are distinctly each others successors. I wish their experience no lesse then mine, and your love to them no lesse then mine to you. But this bruit from Nandsamund, that you are come to destroy my Coun-try, so much affrighteth all my people as they dare not visit you. What will it availe you to take that by force you may quickly have by love, or to destroy them that provide you food[?]. What can you get by warre, when we can hide our provisions and fly to the woods? whereby you must famish by wronging us your friends. And why are you thus jealous of our loves seeing us unarmed, and both doe, and are willing still to feede you, with that you cannot get but by our labours? Thinke you I am so simple, not to know it is better to eate good meate, lye well, and sleepe quietly with my women and children, laugh and be merry with you, have copper, hatchets, or what I want being your friend: then be forced to flie from all, to lie cold in the woods, feede upon Acornes, rootes, and such trash, and be so hunted by you, that I can neither rest, eate, nor sleepe; but my tyred men must watch, and if a twig but breake, every one cryeth there commeth Captaine Smith: then must I fly I know not whether: and thus with miser-able feare, end my miserable life, leaving my pleasures to such youths as you, which through your rash unad-visednesse may quickly as miserably end, for want of that, you never know where to finde. Let this therefore assure you of our loves, and every yeare our friendly trade shall furnish you with Corne; and now also, if you would come in friendly manner to see us, and not thus with your guns and swords as to invade your foes.

Source: Library of Congress, at http://www.loc.gov/teachers/classroommaterials/presentationsandactivities/presentations/timeline/colonial/indians/exchange.html

DRAWING CONCLUSIONS:

1. Based on what you know about Powhatan-English relations, particularly between John Smith and the Powhatans, how credible do you find Smith's account of this speech?

2. If accepted as essentially faithful to Powhatan's views, what does this speech suggest about Powhatan's strategy for dealing with Smith and the English?

1.6   ENGLISH ACCOUNTS OF JAMESTOWN'S "STARVING TIME" (1610)

As John Smith had been the most effective English leader at negotiating with the Powhatans for food and safety, his departure in October 1609 (after a gunpowder accident) seriously damaged the infant colony's prospects. The winter between his departure and the arrival of Thomas Gates in May of 1610 (after being delayed for several months due to a ship wreck at Bermuda) was especially deadly and became known as the "Starving Time."

GUIDING QUESTIONS:

1. According to Simmons, how did the English relations with the Powhatans shift after Smith's departure?
2. What was the state of English-Powhatan relations in 1610, according to these two accounts?

WILLIAM SIMMONS, DOCTOR OF DIVINITY, 1610

The day before Captaine Smith returned for England with the ships, Captaine Davis arrived in a small Pinace, with some sixteene proper men more: To these were added a company from James towne, under the command of Captaine John Sickelmore alias Ratliffe, to inhabit Point Comfort. Captaine Martin and Captaine West, having lost their boats and neere halfe their men among the Salvages, were returned to James towne; for the Salvages no sooner understood Smith was gone, but they all revolted, and did spoile and murther all they incountered. Now wee were all constrained to live onely on that Smith had onely for his owne Companie, for the rest had consumed their proportions, and now they had twentie Presidents with all their appurtenances: Master Piercie our new President, was so sicke hee could neither goe nor stand. But ere all was consumed, Captaine West and Captaine Sickelmore, each with a small ship and thirtie or fortie men well appointed, sought abroad to trade. Sickelmore upon the confidence of Powhatan, with about thirtie others as carelesse as himselfe, were

all slaine, onely Jeffrey Shortridge escaped, and Pokahontas the Kings daughter saved a boy called Henry Spilman, that lived many yeeres after, by her meanes, amongst the Patawomekes. Powhatan still as he found meanes, cut off their Boats, denied them trade, so that Captaine West set saile for England. Now we all found the losse of Captaine Smith, yea his greatest maligners could now curse his losse: as for corne, provision and contribution from the Salvages, we had nothing but mortall wounds, with clubs and arrowes; as for our Hogs, Hens, Goats, Sheepe, Horse, or what lived, our commanders, officers & Salvages daily consumed them, some small proportions sometimes we tasted, till all was devoured; then swords, armes, pieces, or any thing, wee traded with the Salvages, whose cruell fingers were so oft imbrewed in our blouds, that what by their crueltie, our Governours indiscretion, and the losse of our ships, of five hundred within six moneths after Captaine Smiths departure, there remained not past sixtie men, women and children, most miserable and poore creatures; and those were preserved for the most part, by roots, herbes, acornes, walnuts, berries, now and then a little fish: they that

Source: Library of Congress, at http://www.loc.gov/teachers/classroommaterials/presentationsandactivities/presentations/timeline/colonial/indians/advantage.html

had startch in these extremities, made no small use of it; yea, even the very skinnes of our horses. Nay, so great was our famine, that a Salvage we slew, and buried, the poorer sort tooke him up againe and eat him, and so did divers one another boyled and stewed with roots and herbs.

A TRUE DECLARATION OF THE STATE OF THE COLONY OF VIRGINIA, 1610

The state of the Colony, by these accidents began to find a sensible declyning: which Powhatan (as a greedy Vulture) obseruing, and boyling with desire of reuenge, he inuited Captaine Ratclife, and about thirty others to trade for Corne, and under the colour of fairest friendship, he brought them within the compasse of his ambush, whereby they were cruelly murthered, and massacred. For vpon confidence of his fidelitie, they went one and one into seuerall houses, which caused their seuerall destructions, when if but any six had remained together, they would haue been a bulwarke for the generall pre-seruation. After this, Powhatan in the night cut off some of our boats, he draue away all the Deere into the farther part of the Countrie, hee and his people destroyed our Hogs (to the number of about sixe hundred) he sent none of his Indians to trade with vs, but laied secret ambushes in the woods, that if one or two dropped out of the fort alone, they were indaungered.

DRAWING CONCLUSIONS:

1. What do these two accounts suggest about changes to Powhatan strategy after the departure of Smith, with whom they had forged a special relationship?
2. Why do you think that Smith's leadership had been so important?

1.7 VIRGINIA COMPANY INSTRUCTIONS TO GOVERNOR THOMAS GATES (1609)

Sir Thomas Gates served as deputy governor and then governor of the struggling Virginia Colony between 1610 and 1613. In addition to establishing a strict system of law to govern the settlers, Gates escalated the conflict with the Powhatans, waging an ongoing war,—often labeled the First Anglo-Powhatan War—that ultimately concluded with the kidnapping of Pocahontas and her eventual marriage to John Rolfe. Gates received these instructions from the Virginia Company in 1609 and began implementing them in 1610, after the departure of John Smith.

GUIDING QUESTION:

1. What are the basic assumptions here about the Native inhabitants of Tsenacommacah?

17. Your enemies can be but of two sortes straungers ["strangers," meaning Europeans, probably Spanish] and natiues, for the first your defence must be vppon advauntage of the place and way vnto it for fortes haue no other vse but that a fewe men may defend and dispute their footing with them against a greater nomb and to winne time. . . . Besides it is not safe to lett any of the Savages dwell betwene you and the Sea—least they be made guides to your enemies. . . .

18. The second enemy is the Natiues who can no way hurte you but by fire or by destroyinge your Catle, or hinderinge your workes by Stealth or your passages in small nombers, and in this sorte of warr, there is most pill [peril?] yf you be not very Carefull, for if they may destroy but one haruest or burne your townes in the night they will leaue you naked and exposed to famine and Cold, and convey themselues into wodes, where revenge wilbe as difficult as vnnecessary to prevent that you must keepe good watches in the fielde and suffer none of them to come nere your corne in those daungerous seasons and continuall centinells without the walles or vttermost defences in the night, and you must giue order that your Catle be kept in heards waited and attended on by some small watch or so enclosed by themselues that they destroy not your corne and other seed provisions:

19. For Powhaton and his Weroances it is Clere even to reason beside our experience that he loued not our neighborhood and therefore you may no way trust him, but if you finde it not best to make him your prisoner yet you must make him your tributary, and all other his weroances about him first to acknowledge no other Lord but Kinge James and so we shall free them all from the Tirrany of Powhaton [space in manuscript] vppon them Euery Lord of a Province shall pay you and send you into your forte where you make your Cheif residence so many measures of Corne at euery Harvest, and many basketts of Dye so many dozens of skins so many of his people to worke weekely, and of vuery thing somewhat, according to his pporccon in greatenes of Territory and men, by which meanes you shall quietly drawe to your selues an annuall revennue of euery Commodity growinge in that Counrey and this tribute payd to you for which you shall deliuer them from the exeaccons of Powhaton, which are now burdensome and ptect and defend them from all their enemies shall also be a meanes of Clearinge much ground of wood and of

Source: Library of Congress, at http://www.loc.gov/teachers/classroommaterials/presentationsandactivities/presentations/timeline/colonial/indians/natives.html. Spellings using superscript letters have been modernized.

reducing them to laboure and trade seinge [for] this rent onely; they shall enioye their howses, and the rest of their travell quietly and many other commodities and blessings of which they are yet insensible:

20. Yf [If] you hope to winne them and to pvide for your selues by trade, you wilbe deceaued for already your Copper is embased by your abundance and neglect of prisinge it, and they will never feede you but for feare. Wherefore if you pceaue [perceive] that they vppon your landinge, fly vp into the Countrey and forsake their habitaccon you must seise into your custody half there corne and harvest and their Weroances and all other their knowne successors at once whom if you intreate well and educate those which are younge and to succeede in the governement in your Manners and Religion, their people will easily obey you and become in time Civill and Christian:

21. Yf you make friendship with any of these nations, as you must doe, Choose to doe it with those that are farthest from you and enemies vnto those amonge whom you dwell for you shall haue least occasion to haue differences with them, and by that meanes a suerer league of Amity[.] And you shalbe suerer of their trade pteley for Covetousnes and to serue their owne ends, where the Copper is yett in his primary estimaccon which Pohaton [Powhatan] hath hitherto engrossed and partely for feare of Constrainte. Monocon to the east and head of our Riuer, Powhatons enemy and the Manahockes to the Northeast to the head of the Riuer of Moyompo in the necke of the land to the west betweene our bay and the sea. Cathcatapeius a greater Weroance then he is, also his enemy to the Southeast and South. he hath no freinde to the North. The Masawoymekes make continuall incursions vppon him and vppon all those that inhabite the Riuers of Bolus and Myomps and to the Northwest. Pocoughtuwonough infecteth him with a Terrible warr, with those you may hold trade and freindeship good Cheape for their emotenes will prevent all offence which must needes happen beweene vs and them which we are mingled with to the north. at the head Bay is a large towne where is store of Copper

and Furres called Cataaneon that trade and discouery wilbe to greate purpose, yf it may be setled yearely:

22. Such trade as you shall finde necessary or pfitable for you with the Indians you shall endeauour to drawe them to seeke of you and to bringe their Commodities into your forte which will greatly ease the imployment of many men, and this you may bringe to passe by seeminge to make litle estimaccon of trade with them, and by pretendinge to be so able to consist within your selues as that you neede care for nothinge of theires, but rather that you doe them a Curtesy to spare such necessaries as they want as leetle Iron tooles or copper or the like such as are convenient for traffique and so one officer or two in euery forte, whome you must onely appointe to be truncmasters may dispatch the whole busines of trade which els will cost you may mens laboures, if you seeke it far from home. And besides these you must by proclamaccon or edicte publiquely affixed prohibite and forbidd vppon paine of punishement of your discreccon all other psons to trade or exchange for anythinge, but such as shalbe necessarie for foode or clothinge and vppon all such commodities of yours as shall passe away from you. . . .

23. You must constitute and declare some sharpe lawe with a penaltie theron to restrayne the trade of any phibited goods especially of Swordes, Pikeheads gunnes Daggers or any thinge of Iron that may be turned against you and in case of such offence punishe severely haue also especially regard that no arte or trade tendinge to armes in any wise as Smythey Carpentry of or such like be taught the Savages or vsed in their Presence as they may learne therein.

DRAWING CONCLUSIONS:

1. What do these instructions reveal about the evolving English strategy for dealing with the Powhatans?
2. How realistic do these instructions seem, given the precarious situation of the English settlement at this time?

1.8   ALEXANDER WHITAKER, *GOOD NEWS FROM VIRGINIA* (LONDON, 1613)

Whitaker was the Anglican minister at Henrico, a settlement near Jamestown, from approximately 1612 to 1614. He addressed this piece to the Virginia Company in July 1612 to defend the colony against its critics, whom he accused of undermining the propagation of the Christian gospel. Whitaker went on to oversee the conversion and baptism of Pocahontas and possibly officiated her marriage to John Rolfe.

GUIDING QUESTIONS:

1. How does Whitaker describe the Native inhabitants of Virginia?
2. On what basis does Whitaker call for both optimism and patience regarding the Virginia Colony?

[L]et the miserable condition of these naked slaves of the devil move you to compassion toward them. They acknowledge that there is a great good God, but know Him not, having the eyes of their understanding as yet blinded; wherefore they serve the devil for fear after a most base manner, sacrificing sometimes (as I have here heard) their own children to him. I have sent one image of their god to the council in England which is painted upon one side of a toadstool, much like unto a deformed monster. Their priests (whom they call Quiokosoughs) are no other but such as our English witches are. They live naked in body, as if their shame of their sin deserved no covering. Their names are as naked as their body. They esteem it a virtue to lie, deceive, and steal, as their master, the devil, teacheth them. Much more might be said of their miserable condition. . . . If this be their life, what, think you, shall become of them after death but to be partakers with the devil and his angels in hell for evermore? Wherefore, my brethren, put on the bowels of compassion and let the lamentable estate of these miserable people enter into your consideration. One God created us; they have reasonable souls and intellectual faculties as well as we; we all have. Adam for our common parent: yea, by nature the condition of us both is all one, the servants of sin and slaves of the devil. Oh, remember (I beseech you) what was the state of England before the Gospel was preached in our country. How much better were we then and concerning our souls' health than these now are? Let the word of the Lord sound out, that it may be heard in these parts; and let your faith which is toward God spread itself abroad, and show forth the charitable fruits of it in these barren parts of the world. "And let him know that he which hath converted a sinner from going astray out of his way shall save a soul from death and hide a multitude of sins."

But if any of us should misdoubt that this barbarous people is uncapable of such heavenly mysteries, let such men know that they are far mistaken in the nature of these men; for beside the promise of God, which is without respect of persons, made as well to unwise men after the flesh as to the wise, etc., let us not think that these men are so simple as some have supposed them. For they are of body lusty, strong, and very nimble: they are a very understanding

Source: Edmund Clarence Stedman and Ellen Mackay Hutchinson, eds., *A Library of American Literature from the Earliest Settlement to the Present Time: Early Colonial Literature, 1607–1764*, Vol. 1 (New York, 1888), 37–39. Spellings have been modernized.

generation, quick of apprehension, sudden in their dispatches, subtle in their dealings, exquisite in their inventions, and industrious in their labor. I suppose the world hath no better marksmen with their bow and arrows than they be; they will kill birds flying, fishes swimming, and beasts running: they shoot also with marvellous strength. They shot one of our men (being unarmed) quite through the body and nailed both his arms to his body with one arrow. One of their children also, about the age of twelve or thirteen years, killed a bird with his arrow in my sight. The service of their God is answerable to their life being performed with great fear and attention and many strange dumb shows used in the same, stretching forth their limbs and straining their body much like to the counterfeit women in England who feign themselves bewitched or possessed of some evil spirit.

They stand in great awe of their Quiokosoughs or priests, which are a generation of vipers even of Satan's own brood. The manner of their life is much like to the popish hermits of our age; for they live alone in the woods, in houses sequestered from the common course of men; neither may any man he suffered to come into their house or to speak with them but when this priest doth call him. He taketh no care for his victuals, for all such kind of things, both bread and water, etc., are brought unto a place near unto his cottage and there are left, which he fetcheth for his proper need. If they would have rain, or have lost any thing, they have their recourse to him who conjureth for them and many times prevaileth. If they be sick, he is their physician; if they be wounded, he sucketh them. At his command they make war and peace, neither do they any thing of moment without him. I will not be tedious in these strange narrations; when I have more perfectly entered into their secrets you shall know all. Finally, there is a civil government amongst them which they strictly observe and show thereby that the law of nature dwelleth in them, for they have a rude kind of commonwealth, and rough government, wherein they both honor and obey their kings, parents, and governors, both greater and less. They observe the limits of their own possessions and encroach not upon their neighbors' dwellings. Murder is a capital crime scarce heard of among them; adultery is most severely punished, and so are their other offences. These unnurtured grounds of reason in them may serve to encourage us to instruct them in the knowledge of the true God, the rewarder of all righteousness, not doubting but that He that was powerful to save us by His word when we were nothing, will be merciful also to these sons of Adam in His appointed time, in whom there be remaining so many footsteps of God's image. . . .

Let then your liberal minds (you honorable and charitable adventurers of Virginia) be stirred up to cast your alms on the waters of Virginia without hope of present profit. The base affections of the usurer will not look for the overplus of increase until the covenanted time of his loan be expired. The husbandman casting his seed into the earth waiteth upon God until harvest for a fruitful crop. Verily he that believeth doth not make haste. Be not overhasty with God; God will not yet reward you, that he may make you more famous in the world, that the world may see your zeal, and bear witness to the patience of your faith, not to greedy haste of covetous desires. The work is honorable and now more than ever sustained by most honorable men. . . .

DRAWING CONCLUSIONS:

1. What were Whitaker's ambitions for changing the Powhatans and other Native people of Virginia?

1.9   EDWARD WATERHOUSE, A DECLARATION OF THE STATE OF THE COLONIE AND AFFAIRES IN VIRGINIA (1622)

This 1622 report on the Powhatan surprise attack against the English on March 22 of that year was prepared by Edward Waterhouse, secretary of the Virginia Company of London. Waterhouse himself, it is important to note, was not present in Virginia at the time of the attacks. Instead, he gathered information from both letters and accounts he heard from colonists who had traveled back to England after the attacks.

GUIDING QUESTION:

1. Why does Waterhouse see the attacks as "good" for the colony?

Thus have you seene the particulars of this massacre . . . wherein treachery and cruelty haue done their worst to vs, or rather to themselues; for whose vnderstanding is so shallow, as not to perceiue that this must needs bee for the good of the Plantation after, and the losse of this blood to make the body more healthfull, as by these reasons may be manifest.

First, because betraying of innocency neuer rests vnpunished . . .

Secondly, Because our hands which before were tied with gentlenesse and fair vsage, are now set at liberty by the treacherous violence of the [Savages], no vntying the knot, but cutting it: So that we, who hitherto haue had possession of no more ground then their waste, and our purchase at a valuable consideration to their owne contentment, gained; may now by right of Warre, and law of Nations, inuade their Country, and destroy them who sought to destroy vs; whereby wee shall enioy their cultiuated places . . . and possessing the fruits of others labours. Now their cleared grounds in all their villages (which are situate in the fruitfullest places of the land) shall be inhabited by vs, whereas heretofore the grubbing of woods was the greatest labour.

Thirdly, Because those commodities which the Indians enioyed as much or rather more than we, shall now also be entirely possessed by vs. The Deere and other beasts will be in safety, and infinitly increase . . . The like may be said of our owne Swine and Goats, whereof they haue vsed to kill eight in tenne more than the English haue done. . . .

Fourthly, Because the way of conquering them is much more easie then of ciuilizing them by faire meanes, for they are a rude, barbarous, and naked people, scattered in small companies, which are helps to Victorie, but hinderances to Ciuilitie: Besides that, a conquest may be of many, and at once; but ciuility is in particular, and slow, the effect of long time, and great industry. Moreouer, victorie of them may bee gained many waies; by force, by surprize, by famine in burning their Corne, by destroying and burning their Boats, Canoes, and Houses . . . By these and sundry other wayes, as by driuing them (when they flye) vpon their enemies, who are round about them, and by aimating and abetting their enemies against them, may their ruine and subiection be soone effected.

Source: Library of Congress, at http://www.loc.gov/teachers/classroommaterials/presentationsandactivities/presentations/timeline/colonial/indians/good.html

So the Spaniard made great vse for his owne turne of the quarrels and enmities that were amongst the Indians, as throughly vnderstanding and following that Maxime of the Politician, *Diude & impera,* Make diuisions and take Kingdomes. . . . In Virginia the many diuers Princes and people there are at this day opposite in infinite factions one vnto another, and many of them beare a mortall hatred to these our barbarous Sauages, that haue beene likely as false and perfidious heretofore to them, as vnto vs of late. So as the quarrels, and the causes of them, and the different humours of these people being well vnderstood, it will be an easie matter to ouerthrow those that now are, or may bee our enemies hereafter, by ayding and setting on their enemies against them. . . .

Fiftly, Because the Indians, who before were vsed as friends, may now most iustly be compelled to seruitude and drudgery, and supply the roome of men that labour, whereby euen the meanest of the Plantation may imploy themselues more entirely in their Arts and Occupations which are more generous, whilest Sauages performe their inferiour workes of digging in mynes, and the like, of whom also some may be sent for the seruice of the Sommer Ilands [Summer Islands].

Sixtly, This will for euer hereafter make vs more cautelous and circumspect, as neuer to bee deceiued more by any other treacheries, but will serue for a great instruction to all posteritie. . . . Hee that trusts not is not deceiued: and make them know that kindnesses are misspent vpon rude natures, so long as they continue rude. . . .

Lastly, We have this benefit more to our comfort, because all good men doe now take much more care of vs then before, since the fault is on their sides, not on ours, who haue vsed so fayre a cariage, euen to our owne destruction. Especially his Maiesties most gratious, tender and paternall care is manifest herein . . .

As also his Royall fauor is amply extended in a large supply of men and other necessaries throughout the whole Kingdome, which are very shortly to bee sent to Virginia. . . .

To conclude then, seeing that Virginia is most abundantly fruitfull, and that this Massacre must rather be beneficiall to the Plantation then impaire it, let all men take courage, and put to their helping hands, since now the time is most seasonable and aduantagious for the reaping of those benefits which the Plantation hath long promised: and for their owne good let them doe it speedily, that so by taking the prioritie of time, they may haue also the priorities of place, in choosing the best Seats of the Country, which now by vanquishing of the Indians, is like to offer a more ample and faire choice of fruitfull habitations, then hitherto our gentlenesse and faire comportment to the Sauages could attaine vnto. . . .

Lastly, it is to be wished, that euery good Patriot will take these things seriously into his thoughts, and consider how deeply the prosecution of this noble Enterprise concerneth the honor of his Maiestie and the whole Nation, the propagation of the Christian Religion, the enlargement, strength, and safety of his Maiesties Dominions, the rich augmenting of his Reuennues [revenues], and imploiment of his Subiects idle at home, the increase of men, Mariners and shipping, and the raising of such necessary commoditie, for the importation of which from forren Countries so great and incredible summes are continually issued and expended. Some may helpe with their purses, some with their persons, some with their fauour, some with their counsell.

DRAWING CONCLUSIONS:

1. Given that Waterhouse's views were widely shared, what did this response mean for the Powhatans?

1.10 JOHN MARTIN, "THE MANNER HOW TO BRING THE INDIANS INTO SUBJECTION" (DEC. 1622)

In this document, John Martin, who was one of the original members of the Virginia Colony's governing council and a prominent landowner, laid out a plan for controlling Virginia's Native population without "making an utter extirpation of them." In the years following the 1622 attack, the colony implemented many of these ideas.

GUIDING QUESTION:

1. On what grounds did Martin argue that the "Indians" should not be eradicated?

THE MANNER HOWE TO BRINGE IN THE INDIANS INTO SUBIECTION WTHOUT MAKINGE AN VTTER EXTERPATION OF THEM TOGETHER WTH THE REASONS

First By disablinge the mayne bodie of the Enemye from haueinge [having] the Sinnewes of all expediccons [necessities]. As namely Corne and all manner of victualls of anye worth.

This is to be acted two manner of wayes.

ffirst by keepeinge them from settinge [setting, meaning planting] Corne at home and fishinge.

Secondly by keepeinge them from their accustomed tradinge for Corne.

For The first it is pformed by haueinge some 200 Souldiers on foote, Contynuallie harrowinge and burneinge all their Townes in wynter, and spoileinge their weares. By this meanes or [our] people seacurely may followe their worke. And yet not to be negligent in keepeinge watch.

For the seacond there must provided some 10 Shallopps [boats], that in May, June, Julye and August may scoure the Baye and keepe the Rivers yt are belonginge to Opichankanoe [Opechancanough].

By this ariseth two happie ends.

ffirst the assured takeinge of great purchases in skynnes [deer skins] and Prisoners.

Seacondly in keepinge them from tradinge for Corne on the Eastern shore and from ye Southward from whence they haue fiue tymes more then they sett them selues.

This Course being taken they haue noe meanes, but must yield to obedience, or flye to borderinge Neighbors who neither will receiue them Nor indeede are able, for they haue but grounds Cleared for their owne use.

The keeping of them from tradeinge wth the Easterne shore prduceth two worthie effects to or exceeding profitt

ffirst or assurance of Corne att all tymes.

Seacondly the ventinge [selling] of much Cloth. . . .

ffor the assured ventinge of Cloth it followeth Consequently two wayes.

ffirst by Varringe [barring?] them of trade for skinns they haueinge none them selues.

Seacondly by the necessite of haueinge clothinge wch by vs shall & may be tendered att all Convenyent tymes.

Reasons why it is not fittinge vtterly to make an exterpation of the Sauages yett. . . .

Source: Library of Congress, at http://www.loc.gov/teachers/classroommaterials/presentationsandactivities/presentations/timeline/colonial/indians/propose.html

Holy writt sayeth . . . not to vtterly distroy the heathen, least [lest] the woods and wilde beasts should ouer runn them.

My owne observaccon hath bene such as assureth me yt if the Indians inhabitt not amongst vs vnder obedience And as they haue ever kept downe ye woods and slayne the wolues, beares, and other beasts . . . we shalbe more opressed in short tyme by their absence, then in their liueing by vs both for or owne securitie as allso for or Cattle.

Seacondly when as by ye meanes before spoken of, they shalbe brought into subiection and shalbe made to deliuer hostriges [hostages] for theire obedience, there is no doubt by gods grace but of the saueinge of many of their soules And then beinge natiues are apter for worke then yet or English are, knowinge howe to attayne greate quantitie of silke, hempe, and flax, and most exquisite in the dressinge thereof ffor or vses fitt for guides vppon discouerye into other Countries adiacent to ours, fitt to rowe in Gallies & friggetts and many other pregnant vses too tedious to sett downe.

Nowe for avoydinge future daynger in or Collonye that may growe Two especiall erevocable lawes are to be made vppon seaueare [severe] penallties.

ffirst yt none of what ranke soeuer doe euer trinke or trade wth in the late prcinct of Opichankanoe nor any borderinge neighbors that ayded him in this last disaster.

Seacondly for or [our] owne people to sett & sowe a sufficient proporccon of corne for their owne vses, and yearely to lay vpp into a granary a pporccon [portion] for wch if they haue noe vse for them selues the next yeare then to be sould and euery man to haue his dewe payd him.

My reason for the first is yt by this meanes the Savages shalbe frustrated of all meanes of buyinge any manner of victualls, and clothinge, but what they shall haue from vs for their labor and industrie . . .

ffor the seacond howe benifitiall the settinge and sowinge of Corne and layinge vpp thereof for store, will luculently appeare by their nowe endureinge want being disturbed by theis Savages at this tyme, And likewise other vnexpected accedents may happen both by forrayne and domesticke enymies hereafter.

DRAWING CONCLUSIONS:

1. What did the harsh tactics that Martin recommended mean for the Powhatans?

1.11 VIRGINIA'S GOVERNOR AND COUNCIL THREATEN REVENGE AGAINST POWHATANS (1629)

Conflict and mistrust simmered for many years after the 1622 surprise attack against the English. This 1629 document provides a window into the ongoing tensions. (The spelling and punctuation have been largely modernized.)

GUIDING QUESTION:

1. What Powhatan offenses did the Virginians perceive, and what might have been the cause or occasion for these offenses?

A COURT AT JAMES CITY, 1629

Present: John Pott, Esq., Governor, etc.; Captain Smyth; Captain Mathewes

At this court was held a serious consultation concerning the massacre of Mr. Pooly and four other of our men with him by the Indians, And at length it was concluded that one of the Indians now remaining with us should be sent unto the great King [Opechancanough] with a message to this effect, *viz.*, that whereas by the last treaty of peace it was agreed on that none of their people should come to any of our plantations or houses nor call or parley with our men, But if any should come a[bout] any special business from the great king they should come to the governor and in other places to the commander only and that they should steal nothing from us, nor kill nor hurt our cattle [among] diverse other things contained in the said treaty since which time an Indian came in contrary to the said agreement who notwithstanding we forbore to kill or punish but sent him back with a [word of] strict warning that none of the Indians what[soever] should presume to come in without the . . . [missing words], and those only to come to the appointed place at *Pasbyhey* which order they have nevertheless not observed, but have come to diverse of our plantations, stolen our hoes, killed our hogs and done us many other wrongs, some of the whom also although we have detained, yet we have not offered them any violence but have used them [i.e., treated them] well and courteously notwithstanding all which they have killed five of our men which we conceive to be by the king's knowledge and consent and therefore we demand satisfaction, which if he refuse to give we determined by force and arms to revenge both [the] death of our mean and repair all other wrongs they have done us.

DRAWING CONCLUSIONS:

1. What does this document reveal about the English attitude toward the Powhatans and other Native people in the decade following the 1622 attack?

Source: H. R. McIwaine, ed., *Minutes of the Council and General Court of Colonial Virginia, 1622–1632, 1670–1676* (Richmond, VA, 1924), 198.

1.12 TREATY BETWEEN VIRGINIA COLONY AND THE POWHATAN INDIANS (1646)

In October of 1646, following the Powhatan attack of 1644, the Virginia General Assembly approved the following treaty between the colony and the fragmented remains of the chiefdom, which was led briefly by Chief Necotowance after Opechancanough's murder while in the custody of the colonial government. The treaty specified that the "Indians" under Necotowance, which seemed to include all of the remaining Native people near English settlements, would become tributaries of the English Crown, giving an annual payment of beaver skins. Additionally, the tribes ceded much territory to the English, including the land between the James and York Rivers, east of the fall line.

GUIDING QUESTION:

1. In addition to tribute requirements and land cessions, what limitations did the Virginians impose on the Powhatans and other Native people remaining in Tsenacommacah?

Art. 1. BE it enacted by this Grand Assembly, That the articles of peace following between the inhabitants of this collony, and Necotowance King of the Indians bee duely & inviolably observed upon the penaltie within mentioned as followeth:

Imp. That Necotowance do acknowledge to hold his kingdome from the King's Ma'tie of England, and that his successors be appointed or confirmed by the King's Governours from time to time, And on the other side, This Assembly on the behalfe of the collony, doth, undertake to protect him or them against any rebells or other enemies whatsoever, and as an acknowledgment and tribute for such protection, the said Necotowance and his successors are to pay unto the King's Govern'r. the number of twenty beaver skins att the goeing away of Geese yearely.

Art. 2. That it shall be free for the said Necotowance and his people, to inhabit and hunt on the north-side of Yorke River, without any interruption from the English. Provided that if hereafter, it shall be thought fitt by the Governor and Council to permitt any English to inhabitt from Poropotanke downewards, that first Necotowance be acquainted therewith.

Art. 3. That Necotowance and his people leave free that tract of land betweene Yorke river and James river, from the falls of both the rivers to Kequotan [a settlement near the mouth of the James River], to the English to inhabitt on, and that neither he the said Necotowance nor any Indians do repaire to or make any abode upon the said tract of land, upon paine of death, and it shall be lawfull for any person to kill any such Indian, And in case any such Indian or Indians being seen upon the said tract of land shall make an escape, That the said Necotowance shall upon demand deliver the said Indian or Indians to the Englishmen, upon knowledge had of him or them, unles such Indian or Indians be sent upon a message from the said Necotowance.

And to the intent to avoid all injury to such a messenger, and that no ignorance may be pretended to such as shall offer any outrage, It is thought fitt and hereby enacted, That the badge worne by a messenger, or, in case there shall be more than one, by

Source: William Waller Hening, ed., *The Statutes at Large; Being a Collection of All the Laws of Virginia from the First Session of the Legislature in the Year 1619*, Vol. 1 (New York, 1814): 323–326.

one of the company, be a coate of striped stuffe which is to be left by the messenger from time to time so often as he shall returne at the places appointed for coming in.

Art. 4. And it is further enacted, That in case any English shall repaire contrary to the articles agreed upon, to the said north side of Yorke river, such persons soe offending, being lawfully convicted, be adjudged as felons; Provided that this article shall not extend to such persons who by stresse of weather are forced upon the said land, Provided alsoe and it is agreed by the said Necotowance, that it may be lawfull for any Englishman to goe over to the said north side haveing occasion to fall timber trees or cut sedge, soe as the said persons have warr't for theyre soe doeing under the hand of the Gov. Provided alsoe notwitstandinge any thing in this act to the contrary, That it shall bee free and lawfull for any English whatsoever between this present day and the first of March next to kill and bring away what cattle or hoggs that they can by any meanes kill or take upon the said north side of the said river.

Art. 5. And it is further enacted that neither for the said Necotowance nor any of his people, do frequent come in to hunt or make any abode nearer the English plantations then the lymits of Yapin the black water, and from the head of the black water upon a straite line to the old Monakin Towne, upon such paine and penaltie as aforesaid.

Art. 6. And it is further ordered enacted that if any English do entertain any Indian or Indians or doe conceale any Indian or Indians that shall come within the said limits, such persons being lawfully convicted thereof shall suffer death as in case of felony, without benefit of clergy, excepted such as shall be authorized thereto by vertue of this act.

Art. 7. And it is further enacted that the said Necotowance and his people upon all occasions of message to the Gov'r. for trade, doe repaire unto the ffort Royall onely on the north side, at which place they are to receive the aforesaid badges, which shall shew them to be messengers, and therefore to be freed from all injury in their passage to the Governor,

upon payne of death to any person or persons whatsoever that shall kill them, the badge being worn by one of the company, And in case of any other affront, the offence to be punished according to the quality thereof, and the trade admitted as aforesaid to the said Necotowance and his people with the commander of the said ffort onely on the north side.

Art. 8. And it is further thought fitt and enacted, that upon any occasion of message to the Gov'r. or trade, The said Necotowance and his people the Indians doe repair to fforte Henery alias Appamattucke fforte, or to the house of Capt. John ffloud, and to no other place or places of the south side of the river, att which places the aforesayd badges of striped stuff are to be and remaine.

Art. 9. And it is further thought fitt and enacted, That Necotowance doe with all convenience bring in the English prisoners, And all such negroes and guns which are yet remaining either in the possession of himselfe or any Indians, and that here deliver upon demand such Indian servants as have been taken prisoners and shall hereafter run away, In case such Indian or Indians shall be found within the limitts of his dominions; provided that such Indian or Indians be under the age of twelve years at theire running away.

Art. 10. And it is further enacted & consented, That such Indian children as shall or will freely and voluntarily come in and live with the English, may remain without breach of the articles of peace provided they be not above twelve yeares old.

Art. 11. And it is further thought fitt and enacted That the several commanders of the fforts and places as aforesaid unto which the said Indians as aforesaid are admitted to repaire, In case of trade or Message doe forthwith provide the said coats in manner striped as aforesaid.

DRAWING CONCLUSIONS:

1. In light of this treaty, how would you evaluate Opechancanough's strategy during the 1620s through the early 1640s?

1.13 NATHANIEL BACON'S "DECLARATION IN THE NAME OF THE PEOPLE" (1676)

In 1675 and 1676, Nathaniel Bacon led an uprising against the Virginia Colony's government, and an indiscriminate war against Virginia's Native inhabitants, in a conflict that became known as Bacon's Rebellion. This document, which hyperbolically claimed to be a "Declaration in the Name of the People" of Virginia, deployed a wide array of complaints about Governor William Berkeley's policies regarding taxation, security, and trade with the region's Native people. The document concluded by demanding that Berkeley and a long list of his supporters surrender themselves or be captured as traitors. Taxes were indeed notoriously high under Berkeley, and a growing population of landless men and struggling small planters filled out Bacon's forces. His supporters included many who were resentful of the Governor's lucrative trade with Native Americans and who felt unprotected from attacks by Native people, who were in turn defending their own lands.

GUIDING QUESTION:

1. In what ways were these grievances a response to the Indian policy of the Virginia government in the late 1600s?

1. For having, upon specious pretenses of public works, raised great unjust taxes upon the commonalty for the advancement of private favorites and other sinister ends, but no visible effects in any measure adequate; for not having, during this long time of his government, in any measure advanced this hopeful colony either by fortifications, towns, or trade. . . .

3. For having wronged his Majesty's prerogative and interest by assuming monopoly of the beaver trade and for having in it unjust gain betrayed and sold his Majesty's country and the lives of his loyal subjects to the barbarous heathen.

4. For having protected, favored, and emboldened the Indians against his Majesty's loyal subjects, never contriving, requiring, or appointing any due or proper means of satisfaction for their many invasions, robberies, and murders committed upon us.

5. For having, when the army of English was just upon the track of those Indians, who now in all places burn, spoil, murder and when we might with ease have destroyed them who then were in open hostility, for then having expressly countermanded and sent back our army by passing his word for the peaceable demeanor of the said Indians, who immediately prosecuted their evil intentions, committing horrid murders and robberies in all places, being protected by the said engagement and word past of him the said Sir William Berkeley, having ruined and laid desolate a great part of his Majesty's country, and have now drawn themselves into such obscure and remote places and are by their success so emboldened and confirmed by their confederacy so strengthened that the cries of blood are in all places, and the terror and consternation of the people so great, are now become not only difficult but a very formidable enemy who might at first with ease have been destroyed. . . .

Source: *Collections of the Massachusetts Historical Society*, 4th series, Vol. IX (Boston, 1871), 184–187. Some spellings have been modernized.

8. For the prevention of civil mischief and ruin amongst ourselves while the barbarous enemy in all places did invade, murder, and spoil us, his Majesty's most faithful subjects.

Of this and the aforesaid articles we accuse Sir William Berkeley as guilty of each and every one of the same, and as one who has traitorously attempted, violated, and injured his Majesty's interest here by a loss of a great part of this his colony and many of his faithful loyal subjects by him betrayed and in a barbarous and shameful manner exposed to the incursions and murder of the heathen. . . .

These are, therefore, in his Majesty's name, to command you forthwith to seize the persons above mentioned as traitors to the King and country and them to bring to Middle Plantation and there to secure them until further order, and, in case of opposition, if you want any further assistance you are forthwith to demand it in the name of the people in all the counties of Virginia.

NATH Bacon
General by Consent of the people.

DRAWING CONCLUSIONS:

1. What does this document suggest about English-Indian relations in the wake of the Virginia Colony's tobacco-fueled expansion?

1.14 TREATY OF MIDDLE PLANTATION (1677)

In the aftermath of Bacon's Rebellion, which included not only an attempted overthrow of the colonial government but also a general war against Virginia's Native people, agents of the Crown negotiated this "Treaty of Middle Plantation" with a dozen of the remaining tribal leaders, including Cockacoeske, the "Queen" of the Pamunkey (one of the tribes in the original Powhatan chiefdom), who was a relative of the late Powhatan. Some punctuation and spelling have been modernized for the purposes of clarity.

GUIDING QUESTION:

1. How did this treaty define the status of Native people within the declared boundaries of the Virginia Colony?

Articles of Peace between the most Mighty Prince, and our Dread Sovereign Lord CHARLES the Second, by the Grace of God, King of Great Britain, France and Ireland, Defender of the Faith, &c. And the several Indian Kings and Queens, &c. Assenters and Subscribers hereunto, made and concluded at the Camp at Middle Plantation the Twenty ninth day of May 1677. being the day of the most happy Birth and Restauration of our said Sovereign Lord, and in the Nine and twentieth Year of His Majesties Reign, By the Right Honourable Herbert Jefferies Esquire, Lieutenant-Governour of His Majesties Colony of Virginia.

Present, The Honourable Sir John Berry Knight, & [The Honourable] Francis Moryson Esq; His most Sacred Majesties Commissioners appointed under the Great Seal of England for the Affairs of Virginia, And The Honourable Council of State of the said Colony.

Whereas his most Sacred Majesty hath His Own Royal Grace and mere Motion Intrusted to my Care and Endeavours the Renewing, Management and Concluding a good Peace with the Neighbour Indians In Order whereunto (with the Advice and Assistance of the Honourable Sir John Berry Knight, and Francis Morison Esquire) I have caused to be drawn up these ensuing Articles and Overtures, for the firm Grounding, and sure Establishment of a good and just Peace with the said Indians. And that it may be a Secure and Lasting one (Founded upon the strong Pillars of Reciprocal Justice) by Confirming to them their Just Rights, and by Redress of their Wrongs and Injuries; That so the great God (who is a God of Peace, and lover of Justice) may uphold and prosper this our Mutual League and Amity, It is hereby Concluded, Consented to, and mutually Agreed, as followeth:

1. First, that the respective Indian Kings and Queens do from henceforth acknowledge to have their immediate Dependency on, and own all Subjection to the Great King of England, our now Dread Sovereign, His Heirs and Successors, when they pay their Tribute to His Majesties Governour for the time being.

2. That thereupon the said Indian Kings and Queens and their Subjects, shall hold their Lands, and have the same Confirmed to them and their Posterity, by Patent under the Seal of this His Majesties Colony, without any Fee, Gratuity or Reward for the same, in such sort, and in as free and firm manner as others His Majesties Subjects have and enjoy their Lands and Possessions, paying yearly for and in lieu of a Quit Rent, or Acknowledgment for the same, only Three Indian Arrows.

Source: *Acts of the Privy Council of England: Colonial Series*, Vol. 1, edited by William Lawson Grant, James Munro, and Almeric William Fitzroy (H.M. Stationery Office, 1908), 733–739.

3. That all Indians who are in Amity with Us, and have not Land sufficient to Plant upon, be (upon Information) forthwith provided for, and Land laid out and Confirmed to them as aforesaid, never to be disturbed therein, or taken from them, so long as they own, keep and maintain their due Obedience and Subjection to His Majesty, His Governour and Government, and Amity and Friendship towards the English.

4. Whereas by the mutual Discontents, Complaints, Jealousies and Fears of English and Indians, occasioned by the Violent Intrusions of divers English into their Lands, forcing the Indians by way of Revenge, to kill the Cattel and Hogs of the English, whereby Offence and Injuries being given and done on both sides, the Peace of this His Majesties Colony hath been much disturbed, and the late unhappy Rebellion by this means (in a great measure) begun and fomented, which hath Involved this Countrey into so much Ruine and Misery: For prevention of which Injuries and evil consequences (as much as possibly we may) for time to come; It is hereby Concluded and Established, That no English shall Seat or Plant nearer then Three miles of any Indian Town; and whosoever hath made, or shall make an Incroachment upon their Lands, shall be removed from thence, and proceeded against as by the former Peace made, when the Honourable Colonel Francis Morison was Governour, and the Act of Assembly grounded thereupon, is Provided and Enacted.

5. That the said Indians be well Secured and Defended in their Persons, Goods and Properties, against all hurts and injuries of the English; and that upon any breach or violation, hereof the aggrieved Indians do in the first place repair and Address themselves to the Governour, acquainting him therewith (without rashly and suddenly betaking themselves to any Hostile course for Satisfaction) who will Inflict such Punishment on the wilful Infringers hereof, as the Laws of England or this Countrey permit, and as if such hurt or injury had been done to any Englishman; which is but just and reasonable, they owning themselves to be under the Allegiance of His most Sacred Majesty.

6. That no Indian King or Queen be Imprisoned without a special Warrant from His Majesties Governour and Two of the Council, and that no other

Indian be Imprisoned without a Warrant from a Justice of Peace, upon sufficient cause of Commitment.

7. That the said Indians have and enjoy their wonted conveniences of Oystering, Fishing, and gathering Tuchahoe, Curtenemons, Wild Oats, Rushes, Puckoone, or anything else (for their natural support) not useful to the English, upon the English Dividends; Always provided they first repair to some Publick Magistrate of good Repute, and inform him of their number and business, who shall not refuse them a Certificate upon this or any other Lawful occasion, so that they make due return thereof when they come back, and go directly home about their business, without wearing or carrying any manner of Weapon, or lodging under any Englishmans dwelling-house one night.

8. That no Foreign Indian be suffered to come to any English Plantation without a friendly neighbor Indian in his company with such Certificate as aforesaid: and no Indian King is to refuse to send a safe Conduct with the Foreigner, upon any Lawful occasion of his coming in, and that no Indian do paint or disguise themselves when they come in.

9. That all Indian Kings and Queens Tributary to the English, having notice of any march of strange Indians near the English Quarters or Plantations, do forthwith repair to some one of the next Officers of the Militia, and acquaint him of their Nation, number, and design, and which way they bend their course.

10. That if necessary, a convenient Party be presently sent out by the next Colonel of the Militia, to Aid, Strengthen and join with our friendly Indians against any Foreign Attempt, Incursion or Depredation upon the Indian Towns.

11. That every Indian fit to bear Arms, of the Neighbouring Nations in Peace with us, have such quantity of Powder and Shot allotted him, as the Right Honourable the Governour shall think sufficient on any occasion, and that such numbers of them be ready to go out with our Forces upon any march against the Enemy, and to receive such Pay for their good Services, as shall be thought fit.

12. That each Indian King and Queen have equal Power to Govern their own People, and none to have greater Power then other, Except the Queen of Pamunkey [Cockacoeske], to whom several scattered

Nations do now again own their ancient Subjection, and are agreed to come in and Plant themselves under her Power and Government; Who with her, are also hereby included into this present League and Treaty of Peace, and are to keep and observe the same towards the said Queen in all things, as her Subjects, as well as towards the English.

13. That no person whatsoever shall entertain or keep any Neighbouring Indian as Servant, or otherwise, but by Licence of the Governour, and to be upon Obligation answerable for all Injuries and Damages by him or them happening to be done to any English.

14. That no English harbour or entertain any Vagrant or Runaway Indian, but convey him home by way of Pass, from Justice to Justice to his own Town, under Penalty of paying so much per day for harbouring him, as by the Law for entertaining of Runaways is recoverable.

15. That no Indian (of those in Amity with us) shall serve for any longer time then English of the like Ages should serve by Act of Assembly, and shall not be sold as Slaves.

16. That every Indian King and Queen in the Month of March every year, with some of their Great Men, shall tender their Obedience to the Right Honourable His Majesties Governour at the place of his Residence, whereever it shall be, and then and there pay the accustomed Tribute of Twenty Beaver Skins to the Governour, and also their Quit-Rent aforesaid, in acknowledgment they hold their Crowns and Lands of the Great King of England.

17. That due care be had and taken that those Indian Kings and Queens, their Great Men and Attendants that come on any Publick Business to the Right Honourable the Governour, Council or Assembly, may be accommodated with Provisions and Houseroom at the Publick Charge, and that no English Subject shall abuse, revile, hurt or wrong them at any time in word or deed.

18. That upon any Discord or Breach of Peace happening to arise between any of the Indians in Amity with the English, upon the first appearance and beginning thereof, and before they enter into any open Acts of Hostility or War one against another, they shall repair to His Majesties Governour, by whose Justice and Wisdom it is concluded such Difference shall be made up and decided, and to whose final Determination the said Indians shall submit and conform themselves.

19. That for the preventing the frequent mischiefs and mistakes occasioned by unfaithful and corrupt Interpreters, and for the more safety, satisfaction, and advantage both of the Indians and English, That there be one of each Nation of our Neighbouring Indians that can already speak, or may become capable of speaking English, admitted together with those of the English, to be their own Interpreters.

20. That the several Indians concluded in this Peace, do forthwith restore to the respective English Parents and Owners all such Children, Servants and Horses, which they have at any time taken from them, and are now remaining with them the said Indians, or which they can make discovery of.

21. That the Trade with the said Indians be continued, limited, restrained or laid open, as shall make best for the Peace and Quiet of the Countrey; upon which Affair the Governour will consult with the Council and Assembly, and conclude thereon at their next meeting.

[The signatures of the five Indian chiefs appended: the Queen of the Pamunkey (Cockacoeske), on behalf of her self and the several Indians under her Subjection; the Queen of Waonoke; the King of the Nottoways; the King of the Nancymond Indians; and Captain John West, son of Cockacoeske.]

DRAWING CONCLUSIONS:

1. What were the implications of this treaty, in terms of the Native people's position within the Virginia Colony, especially with regard to landholdings?

2. What provisions did the signatory tribes make to protect their own interests?

1.15 ROBERT BEVERLY'S ESTIMATE OF VIRGINIA'S NATIVE POPULATION (C. 1705)

In his *History and Present State of Virginia* (1705), Robert Beverly presented the following description of the size and condition of Virginia's Native population.

GUIDING QUESTION:

1. How does Beverly describe the situation and condition of Virginia's Native population?

The Indians of Virginia are almost wasted, but such towns or people as retain their names and live in bodies are hereunder set down, all which together can't raise five hundred fighting men. They live poorly, and much in fear of the neighboring Indians. Each town, by the articles of peace, 1677, pays three Indian arrows for their land, and twenty beaver skins for protection every year.

In Accomac are eight towns, viz:

Metomkin is much decreased of late by the small pox, that was carried thither.

Gingoteague. The few remains of this town are joined with a nation of the Maryland Indians.

Kiequotank is reduced to very few men.

Matchopungo has a small number yet living.

Occahanock has a small number yet living.

Pungoteague. Governed by a queen, but a small nation.

Onancock has but four or five families.

Chiconessex has very few, who just keep the name.

Nanduye. A seat of the empress. Not above twenty families, but she hath all the nations of this shore under tribute.

In Northampton, Gangascoe, which is almost as numerous as all the foregoing nations put together.

In Prince George Wyanoke is extinct.

In Charles City Appomattox is extinct.

In Surry. Nottawayes, which are about a hundred bowmen, of late a thriving and increasing people.

By Nansemond. Meherrin has about thirty bowmen, who keep at a stand.

Nansemond. About thirty bowmen. They have increased much of late.

In King William's county two. Pamunky has about forty bowmen, who decrease.

Chickahominy, which had about sixteen bowmen, but lately increased.

In Essex. Rappahannock extinct.

In Richmond. Port Tobacco extinct.

In Northumberland. Wiccomocca has but few men living, which yet keep up their kingdom and retain their fashion, yet live by themselves, separate from all other Indians, and from the English.

Thus I have given a succinct account of the Indians; happy, I think, in their simple state of nature, and in their enjoyment of plenty, without the curse of labor. They have on several accounts reason to lament the arrival of the Europeans, by whose means they seem to have lost their felicity as well as their innocence. The English have taken away great part of their country, and consequently made everything less plentiful amongst them. They have introduced drunkenness and luxury amongst them, which have multiplied their wants, and put them upon desiring a

Source: Robert Beverly, *The History of Virginia*, with an introduction by Charles Campbell (J. W. Randolph: Richmond, VA, 1855), 183–185. Reprint of Beverly's *History and Present State of Virginia*, 2nd ed. (London, 1722). Some spellings and punctuation have been modernized.

thousand things they never dreamt of before. I have been the more concise in my account of this harmless people, because I have inserted several figures, which I hope have both supplied the defect of words, and rendered the descriptions more clear. I shall, in the next place, proceed to treat of Virginia as it is now improved (I should rather say altered,) by the English, and of its present constitution and settlement.

DRAWING CONCLUSIONS:

1. What had happened to the Powhatans and their descendants, within a century of the English arrival at Jamestown?

1.16   LINWOOD "LITTLE BEAR" CUSTALOW AND ANGELA L. DANIEL "LITTLE STAR," "THE COLONY SAVED BY THE POWHATAN" (2007)

Although this historical narrative draws on many published sources, its distinctive point of view derives from the oral tradition of the Mattaponi, one of the original six tribes that formed the Powhatan chiefdom. Linwood "Little Bear" Custalow explains in his preface that he learned this story as part of his tribe's "sacred oral history" which was passed down over the generations by Mattaponi *quiakros* ("priests") and chiefs. (For this reason, it is included here as a primary source, even though its perspective is also informed by secondary sources.) Custalow and his coauthor, Angela L. Daniel "Little Star," who was a doctoral student in anthropology at the College of William & Mary when she helped to write this book, describe how according to the Mattaponi oral tradition, Pocahontas's previously unidentified mother was from the Mattaponi tribe. The Mattaponi version of the story includes some disturbing details not contained in previous written accounts, including the claims that Pocahontas was raped in captivity (and was already pregnant at the time of her marriage to John Rolfe) and that she believed that poison caused the sudden illness that led to her death in England in 1617.

GUIDING QUESTIONS:

1. How is the oral tradition on which this account is based a different kind of primary source from the written documents used by other scholars?
2. What claims do the authors make about Pocahontas's marriage to John Rolfe?

THE COLONY SAVED BY THE POWHATAN

After John Rolfe and Pocahontas were married, the Powhatan *quiakros* (priests) made another attempt to appease the English colonists. The Powhatan *quiakros* became friendlier to the settlers, and especially to Rolfe. The leaders among the English colonists had hoped this would happen. They wanted to capture Pocahontas in order to gain more information on how the Powhatan priests processed tobacco. After his marriage to Pocahontas, Rolfe sought counsel from the Powhatan *quiakros* on curing his tobacco crop.

Rolfe left England to come to the colony in the spring of 1609. His goal was to make a profit growing and processing tobacco. On the way, he was shipwrecked in Bermuda, so Rolfe and his English wife did not arrive at the Jamestown colony until a year later, in the spring of 1610.

Rolfe had been unsuccessful at growing and processing tobacco for nearly three years prior to Pocahontas's kidnapping. The *quiarkros* would not reveal Powhatan knowledge regarding tobacco production to him. Rolfe was becoming frustrated. He knew he would have to become successful soon or the entire economic venture in the "New World" would be in jeopardy.

Source: Linwood "Little Bear" Custalow and Angela L. Daniel "Little Star," "The Colony Saved by the Powhatan," from *The True Story of Pocahontas: The Other Side of History* (Golden, CO: Fulcrum Publishing, 2007), 71–77.

The year 1616 was the deadline for the initial investments in the Virginia colony.[1] If results were not produced, the authorization from the British royalty as well as the financial backing from individual investors could be withdrawn. Time was running out for the investment company, the Virginia Company of London, to generate returns. The English colony was on the verge of collapsing from lack of financial profit. Rolfe was linked directly with this company. If it withdrew from financing the colony, Rolfe would have to return to England due to the failure of the colony. To a great extent, the English colony's survival depended upon the success of Rolfe's tobacco and/or the public relations tour in England, which Rolfe and his wife, Pocahontas, were to participate in. The Powhatan people were not aware of the 1616 deadline, but they did know that the colony was failing.

There may have been various reasons that the British Crown chartered the Jamestown colony, perhaps to find a water route to East India or perhaps to prevent the Spaniards from spreading Catholicism throughout the New World.[2] Certainly the reasons of individual colonists varied even more so, such as religious freedom. But ultimately the colony was a business venture sponsored not by the British Crown, but by individuals seeking profitable financial returns. Conditions of this business investment company mandated that such returns would be evident by 1616. The Powhatan, including the *quiakros*, Chief Powhatan Wahunsenaca, and Pocahontas, did not know these details. When they first met, Captain John Smith had told Wahunsenaca that the English were trying to escape from the Spaniards.[3]

One of the first hopes the English had for riches was to find gold. It was believed that Virginia was laden with silver and gold, as the Spaniards had found gold and silver in South America. The immigration to the New World was the English gold rush of the seventeenth century. One motto of the colonists was "No talk, no hope, no work; but dig gold, wash gold, refine gold, load gold."[4] The frenzy for silver and gold often prevailed over levelheadedness. The colonists eagerly loaded one ship "with sand that glistened" before Smith could stop them and persuade them to send a cargo of cedar logs back to England instead.[5]

The planned search for gold was one of the reasons the English colonists had not come prepared to be self-sufficient. They came with the intention of obtaining food from the Native people.[6] Their primary objective was to find gold. When gold or other precious metals were not found, they began to try other means of making money, such as glassmaking and timber harvesting. Time was ticking away while one scheme to turn a profit after the next failed. In addition to mining gold and silver, the Spaniards had been successful in growing tobacco. It was only a matter of time before the English colonists undertook the same business enterprise. The Virginia Company of London made arrangements with Rolfe to pursue such an endeavor.

When Rolfe and his English wife arrived in Jamestown in 1610, he immediately focused his attention on growing tobacco. (His wife died sometime later for unknown and undocumented reasons.) By 1612, Rolfe's first crop was curing. It was taller than the Powhatan

---

1   W. Stitt Robinson Jr., *Mother Earth: Land Grants in Virginia, 1607–1699* (Baltimore: Clearfield, 1957), 14–15. Robinson noted, "Both adventurer and planter were promised a proportionate share of any dividends distributed, whether in land or in money. The joint-stock arrangement was originally set to continue seven years from its inception in 1609, thus making 1616 as the terminal date. During this period monetary dividends might be declared, and at the end of the period the land suitable for cultivation was to be divided with at least 100 acres to be given for each share of stock."

2   W. M. Clark, ed., *Colonial Churches in the Original Colony of Virginia*, 2nd ed. (Richmond, VA: Southern Churchman Company, 1908).

3   John Smith, "A True Relation" in *Jamestown Narratives: Eyewitness Accounts of the Virginia Colony, the First Decade: 1607–1617*, ed. Edward Wright Haile (Champlain, VA: RoundHouse, 2001), 161.

4   Julian Alvin Carroll Chandler and T. B. Thames, *Colonial Virginia* (Richmond, VA: Times-Dispatch, 1907), 35.

5   Ibid.

6   Ibid, 40.

type of tobacco and showed promise.[7] A few hundred pounds were shipped to England on the *Elizabeth* for trial. The prospect of a successful tobacco industry excited the colonists. They were beginning to have hope in finding a successful means of producing financial returns for the investors in the colony. Late in 1613, after the abduction of Pocahontas, Rolfe received word that his tobacco had begun to be compared favorably with the best Spanish leaf, but it was still not good enough be competitive with the Spanish tobacco. After Rolfe married Pocahontas in the spring of 1614, Sir Thomas Dale gave an extensive tract of land in Henrico to Rolfe.[8]

Rolfe's problems in competing with the Spanish tobacco appeared to stem from lack of knowledge and care in curing the tobacco.[9] According to Mattaponi sacred oral history, the Native people of the New World possessed the knowledge of how to cure and process tobacco successfully. The Spanish gained this knowledge from the Native communities they had subdued.

In the Powhatan society, it was the *quiakros* who possessed the knowledge of how to cure tobacco. Powhatan people planted and tended to the crops, but the *quiakros* cured it.

The Powhatan tobacco was harsher and had a strong bite, making it difficult to inhale deeply. Rolfe used the West Indies tobacco seed, which was much milder to inhale. It was not the objective of the Powhatan to smoke tobacco for pleasure, like the English colonists did. Instead, the Powhatan used tobacco primarily for religious and ceremonial activities. Because of the spiritual quality and reference tobacco had in the Powhatan society, it was the *quiakros* who maintained the knowledge of the final steps of processing it. It was not common knowledge, but knowledge held by the elite. As such, somehow Rolfe needed to access and establish good relations with the Powhatan *quiakros* in order to obtain this Native knowledge.

The solution to Rolfe's challenge to establish good relations with the *quiakros* was to marry Pocahontas. Kinship ties were a very important element in the fabric of Powhatan culture and society. Remember, it was the concept of kinship ties that provided meaning and honor to the obligatory marriages of the Paramount chief and women from the alliance tribes. The purpose of this type of marriage was not for love or a lifetime commitment; instead, it was to build and seal bonds through kinship relations.

Rolfe's problems with tobacco were resolved when the Powhatan *quiakros* accepted Rolfe as their friend because he was married to the paramount chief's daughter. You have to remember, most of the *quiakros* were relatives of Pocahontas. The *quiakros* taught Rolfe Powhatan skills in curing and managing tobacco. They hoped this would satisfy the desires of the English colonists and make them happy so that they would ally themselves with the Powhatan nation. As a result of Rolfe being counseled by the Powhatan *quiakros* as to the best methods of successfully curing tobacco in the New World,[10] Rolfe's tobacco improved to rival any tobacco grown by the Spanish.[11]

In the spring of 1616, a ship named the *Treasurer* set sail for England from the Virginia colony. The voyage was arranged by the Virginia Company of London, which had financed the Jamestown settlement. Samuel Argall, Pocahontas's captor, was the captain of the ship. The primary voyagers were Dale, Rolfe, Pocahontas, and her small son, Thomas.[12] Also on board were nearly a dozen Powhatan,[13] including

---

7   The Jamestown Foundation, *The Story of John Rolfe, Who Saved a Colony and Planted the Seeds of a Nation*, Published to commemorate the 350th anniversary of John Rolfe's first harvest (Williamsburg, VA: Jamestown Foundation, 1957), 6.

8   Ibid, 9.

9   Ibid, 6.

10 Jamestown Foundation, n 7, 7. *The Story of John Rolfe* states that it is likely that Pocahontas provided Powhatan knowledge of tobacco management to Rolfe.

11 Ibid, 11.

12 Helen C. Rountree, *Pocahontas's People: The Powhatan Indians of Virginia through Four Centuries* (Norman: University of Oklahoma Press, 1990), 299. Roundtree states in endnote number 67 that Thomas Rolfe was born prior to the voyage to England in 1616. However, the actual date of Thomas Rolfe's birth was not recorded.

13 Ibid, 62.

Mattachanna and Uttamattamakin.[14] Mattachanna cared for Pocahontas, while Uttamattamakin attended to the needs of Rolfe. Other *quiakros* accompanied the voyage in disguise as Powhatan warriors. In order to gain information, the *quiakros* often hid their status from the English colonists by wearing a different type of clothing. The *quiakros* had a distinctive way of dressing, which the English had quickly become aware of and could easily recognize. Although the English colonists never fully grasped the governmental structure of the Powhatan nation, they had recognized the importance of the *quiakros* within the Powhatan society.[15] They considered the *quiakros* a greater threat than the village chiefs. Uttamattamakin, on the other hand, openly conversed among the English colonists as a Powhatan priest. While in England, he openly criticized the English colonists.[16]

The primary cargo on this voyage consisted of Rolfe's tobacco. The success of the tobacco, cured with the help of the Powhatan, was the English colonists' last chance to save the colony financially. In a letter to England prior to their departure, Dale described the crop as "exceedingly good tobacco."[17] It was a critical time for the English colony, but Dale, Argall, and Rolfe—prominent men in the Jamestown colony—were returning to England with a load of promising tobacco and Wahunsenaca's daughter. The voyage conveyed to the royalty in England—and perhaps to the colonists as well—the impression that all was well between the Powhatan people and the English colonists.

Upon their arrival in England, Rolfe's tobacco—which had been grown on the Powhatan land with the help of the Powhatan *quiakros*—surpassed the taste and flavor of the Spanish tobacco. It was a

success. The Virginia Company quickly assessed the profitability of tobacco in the new colony. Refinancing the Virginia colony would come easily now. With financial worries eased, the presence of Pocahontas, the daughter of Wahunsenaca, was even more of a festive occasion. To England, all must have seemed well with the development of the English colony.

The Powhatan actually saved the colony by sharing their knowledge of tobacco curing and management. This sharing of knowledge was directly linked to Wahunsenaca and his daughter, Pocahontas. It was directly related to Wahunsenaca because he had wanted to be friends, at peace, in alliance with the English from the beginning. This provided another opportunity to try to make that agenda work. It was related directly to Pocahontas because she was held in such high favor because of her father, who was the paramount chief. She was married to Rolfe, the English colonist interested in growing tobacco. In addition, many of the *quiakros* were relatives of Pocahontas. If they could, the *quiakros* wanted to make a good relationship out of the devastating events that had occurred. Both the actions taken by individuals and underlining Powhatan cultural persuasions were in play, affecting the responses and actions of the people involved. The deep parental affection Wahunsenaca had for his daughter is always evident throughout Mattaponi sacred oral history.

However, the efforts of the Powhatan *quiakros* had the opposite effects they had hoped for. Instead of the English colonists embracing the Powhatan people and becoming their allies, the colonists' greed was unleashed. Settlers in Jamestown and the surrounding plantations rushed to obtain more Powhatan land to grow tobacco. To a great extent, the search

---

14 John Smith, "The Generall Historie of Virginia," in *The Complete Works of Captain John Smith (1580–1631)*, ed. Philip L. Barbour (Chapel Hill: University of North Carolina Press, 1986), 261.

15 William Strachey, *The Historie of Travaile into Virginia Britinia (1612)* (London: The Hakluyt Society, 1849), 100: "When they [the Powhatan Indians] intend any warrs, the weroances usually advise with their priests or conjurers, their allies and best trusted chouncellors and friends; but commonly the priest have the resulting voice, and determyne therefore their resolutions."

16 Uttamatomakkin (Tomocomo), "An Interview in London" in *Jamestown Narratives: Eyewitness Accounts of the Virginia Colony, the First Decade: 1607–1617*, ed. Edward Wright Haile (Champlain, VA: RoundHouse, 2001), 880–883.

17 Jamestown Foundation, *Story of John Rolfe*, 9.

for gold was forgotten. Tobacco became like gold to the English colonists. It eventually became a form of currency in the Virginia colony.[18] Settlers extended the boundaries of their communities by grabbing the already cleared land of the Powhatan to grow their own tobacco. It was difficult to clear huge trees—the tree logs, the tree limbs, tree stumps, and roots—then prepare the soil to make it suitable to grow tobacco plants. This would have taken the colonists many years; the colonists did not want to wait. So they coveted the Powhatan tribes' open, fertile fields even more so. The English colonists took more and more Powhatan land by force, killing and enslaving larger numbers of Powhatan people. Tobacco was so profitable, every little bit of open space was used to plant it. It was also so profitable that Dale passed a mandate that required every farmer to grow enough corn for subsistence instead of only growing tobacco.[19]

DRAWING CONCLUSIONS:

1. How do the authors describe Powhatan's diplomatic strategy during the 1610s?
2. How does this description differ from the impression left by the the written documentation of the English settlers?

---

18 William Waller Hening, *The Statutes at Large; Being a Collection of All the Laws of Virginia from the First Session of the Legislature in the Year 1619, Vol. 1* (New York: R. & W. & G. Bartow, 1823).

19 Smith, "A True Relation," in *Jamestown Narratives*, 871–872.

CASE STUDY 1: DID POCAHONTAS RESCUE JOHN SMITH FROM EXECUTION?

In his 1624 *Generall Historie of Virginia*, John Smith for the first time gave a detailed account of how Pocahontas had rescued him in 1607 from execution after he had been captured and brought before Chief Powhatan. (His first mention of the incident in print was in the revised 1622 edition of *New England's Trials*.[1]) In the *Generall Historie*, Smith also published an alleged 1616 letter that he had written to Queen Anne, which seemed to corroborate his story. This story, made public several years after the deaths of both Pocahontas and Powhatan, has become one of the most famous episodes in early American history. The story also raises important questions about the Powhatans' initial response to the establishment of the Virginia settlement. Over the years, the incident has been deployed as an emblem of the capitulation of the Powhatans (through Pocahontas) to the presumably more civilized English. In fact, the rescue scene is twice depicted in the Rotunda of the United States Capitol building, in both an 1825 relief sculpture and a late 1870s frieze painting. Further reinforcing the idea of the Powhatans' voluntary subordination to the English is John Gadsby Chapman's oil painting depicting the baptism of Pocahontas, which was placed in the Capitol Rotunda in 1840. The actual event took place in 1614, prior to her marriage to John Rolfe—a union that was apparently approved by Chief Powhatan.

Historians have advanced a variety of interpretations of the rescue described by Smith. The minority position is that this event took place basically as Smith described it. English professor Leo Lemay, for example, is one of a few modern scholars to accept Smith's account. Lemay argues that all available written documents corroborate Smith's account and that Smith was "remarkably consistent . . . over a long period of time."[2] Historian Philip Barbour has suggested another possibility: that Smith experienced (and was misled by) an adoption ritual that included a "mock execution."[3] Historical anthropologist Helen

---

1 John Smith, *New Englands Trials: Declaring the successe of 80 ships employed thither within these eight yeares ; and the benefit of that countrey by sea and land. With the present estate of that happie plantation, begun but by 60 weake men in the yeare 1620. And how to build a fleete of good shippes to make a little nauie royall. Written by Captaine Iohn Smith, sometimes Gouernour of Virginia, and Admirall of New England*. 2nd edition. London: William Jones, 1622.

2 For a summary of this position, see A. Leo Lemay, *Did Pocahontas Save Captain John Smith?* (Athens: University of Georgia Press, 1992), 98–101, especially 100.

3 Philip L. Barbour, *Pocahontas and Her World* (Boston: Houghton Mifflin, 1970), 24–25.

Rountree, however, argues that Smith's account simply does not fit what we know about Powhatan cultural conventions regarding execution or adoption.[4] Both Rountree and historian Camilla Townsend argue that Smith simply invented the story to bolster reader interest. In addition to considering the Powhatan cultural context—in which there is no record of prisoners of war being clubbed to death—Townsend also notes that Smith had a habit of telling tales of being rescued by beautiful women.[5] Nonetheless, both Townsend and Rountree support the idea that Powhatan, in Townsend's words, "ritually adopt[ed]" Smith to establish "kinship ties" for the purposes of securing Smith as a subordinate ally.[6]

The primary sources assembled here provide an opportunity to weigh the reliability of Smith's account that Pocahontas rescued him. Beyond that, however, the entire episode (with all of its uncertainties and ambiguities) offers insights into how the Powhatan responded to the opportunities and perils raised by their contact with John Smith and other English colonizers.

GUIDING QUESTIONS:

1. How credible is Smith's account of being rescued by Pocahontas?
2. Whether Smith was rescued by Pocahontas or not, why do you think that Powhatan decided to spare Smith's life?
3. How does the debate over the rescue story help us better understand the Powhatan strategy for managing the arrival of the English to Tsenacommacah?

---

4   Helen Rountree, *Pocahontas, Powhatan, and Opechancanough: Three Indian Lives Changed by Jamestown* (Charlottesville: University of Virginia Press, 2006), 67–85.
5   Camilla Townsend, *Pocahontas and the Powhatan Dilemma* (New York: Hill & Wang, 2005), 44–65; see especially 56.
6   Ibid. 56.

2.1 ACCOUNTS OF JOHN SMITH'S DECEMBER 1607 CAPTIVITY (1607 & 1624)

The first brief account following comes from Governor Edward-Maria Wingfield's account of Smith's capture by the Pamunkey tribe (part of the Powhatan chiefdom) in December 1607. Although Wingfield's narrative does not mention that Smith was nearly executed, it is possible that this information was intentionally omitted.

The second account comes from Smith's *Generall Historie of Virginia*, which was published in 1624, many years after the event (and several years after the deaths of both Pocahontas and Powhatan). Note that Smith refers to himself in the third person, which was a literary convention of the time.

GUIDING QUESTIONS:

1. How are these two reports consistent?
2. In what ways are they inconsistent? What factors might explain the differences?

GOVERNOR EDWARD-MARIA WINGFIELD'S REPORT, 1607

Decem.—The 10th of December, Mr Smyth went vp the ryuer of the Chechohomynies to trade for corne. He was desirous to see the heade of that riuer; and, when it was not passible wth the shallop, he hired a cannow and an Indian to carry him up further. The river the higher grew worse and worse. Then hee went on shoare wth his guide, and left Robinson & Emmery, twoe of our Men, in the cannow; wch were presently slayne by the Indians, Pamaonke's [Opechancanough's] men, and hee himself taken prysoner, and, by the means of his guide, his lief was saved; and Pamaonché, haueing him prisoner, carryed him to his neybors wyroances to see if any of them knew him for one of those wch had bene, some twoe or three yeeres before vs, in a river amongst them Northward, and taken awaie some Indians from them

by force. At last he brought him to the great Powaton (of whome before wee had no knowledg), who sent him home to our towne the viijth [seventh] of January.

JOHN SMITH'S NARRATIVE OF HIS CAPTIVITY, 1624

The next voyage hee proceeded so farre that with much labour by cutting of trees in sunder he made his passage, but when his Barge could passe no farther, he left her in a broad bay out of danger of shot, commanding none should goe a shore till his returne: himselfe with two English and two Salvages went up higher in a Canowe, but hee was not long absent, but his men went a shore, whose want of government, gave both occasion and opportunity to the Salvages to surprise one George Cassen, whom they slew, and much failed not to have cut of the boat and all the rest.

Sources: "Wingfield's Report" (1607) from the Library of Congress, at http://www.loc.gov/teachers/classroommaterials/presentationsandactivities/presentations/timeline/colonial/indians/captured.html

John Smith, *The Generall Historie of Virginia, New England & the Summer Isles, together with the True Travels, Adventures and Observations, and A Sea Grammar*, Vol. 1, ch. 2. (1624). Reprint (New York: Macmillan, 1907) from the Library of Congress, at https://lccn.loc.gov/75320262.

Smith little dreaming of that accident, being got to the marshes at the rivers head, twentie myles in the desert, had his two men shine [slain] (as is supposed) sleeping by the Canowe, whilst himselfe by fowling sought them victuall, who finding he was beset with 200. Salvages, two of them hee slew, still defending himselfe with the ayd of a Salvage his guid, whom he bound to his arme with his garters, and used him as a buckler, yet he was shot in his thigh a little, and had many arrowes that stucke in his cloathes but no great hurt, till at last they tooke him prisoner. When this newes came to James towne, much was their sorrow for his losse, fewe expecting what ensued. Six or seven weekes those Barbarians kept him prisoner, many strange triumphes and conjurations they made of him, yet hee so demeaned himselfe amongst them, as he not onely diverted them from surprising the Fort, but procured his owne libertie, and got himselfe and his company such estimation amongst them, that those Salvages admired him more then their owne Quiyouckosucks. The manner how they used and delivered him, is as followeth.

The Salvages having drawne from George Cassen whether Captaine Smith was gone, prosecuting that opportunity they followed him with 300 bowmen, conducted by the King of Pamaunkee, who in divisions searching the turnings of the river, found Robinson and Emry by the fire side, those they shot full of arrowes and slew. Then finding the Captaine, as is said, that used the Salvage that was his guide as his shield (three of them being shine and divers other so gauld) all the rest would not come neere him. Thinking thus to have returned to his boat, regarding them, as he marched, more then his way, slipped up to the middle in an oasie creeke & his Salvage with him, yet durst they not come to him till being neere dead with cold, he threw away his armes. Then according to their composition they drew him forth and led him to the fire, where his men were slaine. Diligently they chafed his benummed limbs. He demanding for their Captaine, they shewed him Opechankanough, King of Pamaunkee, to whom he gave a round Ivory double compass Dyall. Much they marvailed at the playing of the Fly and Needle, which they could see so plainely, and yet not touch it, because of the glasse that covered them. But when he demonstrated by that Globe-like Jewell, the roundnesse of the

earth, and skies, the spheare of the Sunne, Moone, and Starres, and how the Sunne did chase the night round about the world continually; the greatnesse of the Land and Sea, the diversitie of Nations, varietie of complexions, and how we were to them Antipodes, and many other such like matters, they all stood as amazed with admiration. Notwithstanding, within an houre after they tyed him to a tree, and as many as could stand about him prepared to shoot him, but the King holding up the Compass in his hand, they all laid downe their Bowes and Arrowes, and in a triumphant manner led him to Orapaks, where he was after their manner kindly feasted, and well used.

Their order in conducting him was thus; Drawing themselves all in fyle, the King in the middest had all their Peeces and Swords borne before him. Captaine Smith was led after him by three great Salvages, holding him fast by each arme: and on each side six went in fyle with their Arrowes nocked. But arriving at the Towne (which was but onely thirtie or fortie hunting houses made of Mats, which they remove as they please, as we our tents) all the women and children staring to behold him, the souldiers first all in fyle performed the forme of a Bissom so well as could be, and on each flanke, officers as Serjeants to see them keepe their orders. A good time they continued this exercise, and then cast themselves in a ring, dauncing in such severall Postures, and singing and yelling out such hellish notes and screeches; being strangely painted, every one his quiver of Arrowes, and at his backe a club; on his arme a Fox or an Otters skinne, or some such matter for his vambrace; their heads and shoulders painted red, with Oyle and Pocones mingled together, which Scarlet-like colour made an exceeding handsome shew; his Bow in his hand, and the skinne of a Bird with her wings abroad dryed, tyed on his head, a peece of copper, a white shell, a long feather, with a small rattle growing at the tayles of their snaks tyed to it, or some such like toy. All this while Smith and the King stood in the middest guarded, as before is said, and after three dances they all departed. Smith they conducted to a long house, where thirtie or fortie tall fellowes did guard him, and ere long more bread and venison was brought him then would have served twentie men, I thinke his stomacke at that time was not very good; what he left they put in baskets and tyed over his head. About midnight they set the meate againe before him, all this time not one of them would eate a bit with him, till the next morning they brought him as much more, and then did they eate all the old, & reserved the new as they had done the other, which made him thinke they would fat him to eate him. Yet in this desperate estate to defend him from the cold, one Maocassater brought him his gowne, in requitall of some beads and toyes Smith had given him at his first arrivall in Virginia.

Two dayes after a man would have slaine him (but that the guard prevented it) for the death of his sonne, to whom they conducted him to recover the poore man then breathing his last. Smith told them that at James towne he had a water would doe it, if they would let him fetch it, but they would not permit that; but made all the preparations they could to assault James towne, craving his advice, and for recompence he should have life, libertie, land, and women. . . .

At last they brought him to Meronocomo [Werowocomoco], where was Powhatan their Emperor. Here more then two hundred of those grim Courtiers stood wondering at him, as he had beene a monster; till Powhatan and his trayne had put themselves in their greatest braveries. Before a fire upon a seat like a bedsted, he sat covered with a great robe, made of Rarowcun skinnes, and all the tayles hanging by. On either hand did sit a young wench of 16 or 18 yeares, and along on each side the house, two rowes of men, and behind them as many women, with all their heads and shoulders painted red; many of their heads bedecked with the white downe of Birds; but every one with something: and a great chayne of white beads about their necks. At his entrance before the King, all the people gave a great shout. The Queene of Appamatuck was appointed to bring him water to wash his hands, and another brought him a bunch of feathers, in stead of a Towell to dry them: having feasted him after their best barbarous manner they could, a long consultation was held, but the conclusion was, two great stones were brought before Powhatan: then as many as could layd hands on him, dragged him to them, and thereon laid his head, and being ready with their clubs, to beate out his braines, Pocahontas the Kings dearest daughter, when no intreaty could prevaile, got his head in her armes,

and laid her owne upon his to save him from death: whereat the Emperour was contented he should live to make him hatchets, and her bells, beads, and copper; for they thought him aswell of all occupations as themselves. For the King himselfe will make his owne robes, shooes, bowes, arrowes, pots; plant, hunt, or doe any thing so well as the rest. . . .

Two dayes after, Powhatan having disguised himselfe in the most fearefull manner he could, caused Capt. Smith to be brought forth to a great house in the woods, and there upon a mat by the fire to be left alone. Not long after from behinde a mat that divided the house, was made the most dolefullest noyse he ever heard; then Powhatan more like a devill then a man with some two hundred more as blacke as himselfe, came unto him and told him now they were friends, and presently he should goe to James towne, to send him two great gunnes, and a gryndstone, for which he would give him the Country of Capahowosick, and for ever esteeme him as his sonne Nantaquoud. So to James towne with 12 guides Powhatan sent him. That night they quarterd in the woods, he still expecting (as he had done all this long time of his imprisonment) every houre to be put to one death or other: for all their feasting. But almightie God (by his divine providence) had mollified the hearts of those sterne Barbarians with compassion. The next morning betimes they came to the Fort, where Smith having used the Salvages with what kindnesse he could, he shewed Rawhunt, Powhatans trusty servant two demi-Culverings [small cannons] & a millstone to carry Powhatan: they found them somewhat too heavie; but when they did see him discharge them, being loaded with stones, among the boughs of a great tree loaded with Isickles, the yce and branches came so tumbling downe, that the poore Salvages ran away halfe dead with feare. But at last we regained some conference with them, and gave them such toyes; and sent to Powhatan, his women, and children such presents, as gave them in generall full content.

DRAWING CONCLUSIONS:

1. Taken on its own, how credible is Smith's story?
2. How does Smith explain his return from captivity to Jamestown?

2.2 JOHN SMITH'S ALLEGED 1616 LETTER TO QUEEN ANNE REGARDING POCAHONTAS (1624)

Smith's *Generall Historie of Virginia*, published in 1624, included the following letter that Smith claimed to have sent to Queen Anne in 1616 to introduce the Queen to Pocahontas during her visit to England. As a primary source, the published letter presents a conundrum because the original letter has not been found. Given that Smith published the letter at the same time that he first published the rescue story, the letter is not very helpful in corroborating the rescue story. Further clouding the water is the fact that Smith introduces the published version as "an abstract," rather than as a duplicate of the original letter. In other words, he purports only to present the letter as he recalled it several years after the fact.

GUIDING QUESTIONS:

1. How does this narrative add to the rescue story that Smith related in his *Generall Historie of Virginia*?
2. The rescue story aside, what might we learn from this source about Powhatan perceptions of the English, based on Smith's description of his interations with Pocahontas and Uttamatomakkin (Tomocomo) in London?

A RELATION TO QUEENE ANNE, OF POCAHONTAS

[S]ome ten yeeres agoe being in *Virginia*, and taken prisoner by the power of *Powhatan* their chiefe King, I receiued from this great Saluage exceeding great courtesie, especially from his sonne *Nantaquaus* the most manliest, comeliest, boldest spirit, I euer saw in a Saluage, and his sister *Pocahontas*, the Kings most deare and wel-beloued daughter, being but a childe of twelue or thirteene yeeres of age, whose compassionate pitifull heart, of my desperate estate, gaue me much cause to respect her: I being the first Christian this proud King and his grim attendants euer saw: and thus inthralled in their barbarous power, I cannot say I felt the least occasion of want that was in the power of those my mortall foes to preuent, notwithstanding al their threats. After some six weeks fatting amongst those Saluage Courtiers, at the minute of my execution, she hazarded the beating out of her owne braines to saue mine, and not onely that, but so preuailed with her father, that I was safely conducted to *Iames* towne [Jamestown], where I found about eight and thirtie miserable poore and sicke creatures, to keepe possession of all those large territories of *Virginia*, such was the weaknesse of this poore Common-Wealth, as had the Saluages not fed vs, we directly had starued [starved].

And this reliefe, most gracious Queene, was commonly brought vs by this Lady *Pocahontas*, notwithstanding all these passages when inconstant Fortune turned our peace to warre, this tender Virgin would still not spare to dare to visit vs, and by her . . . our wants still supplyed; were it the policie of her father thus to imploy her, or the ordinance of God thus to make her his instrument, or her extraordinarie

Source: John Smith, *The Generall Historie of Virginia, New England, and the Summer Isles* (1624); Reprint (Richmond, VA, 1819), 29–33.

affection to our Nation, I know not: but of this I am sure; when her father with the vtmost of his policie and power, sought to surprize mee, hauing but eighteene with mee, the darke night could not affright her from comming through the irkesome woods, and with watered eies gaue me intelligence, with her best aduice to escape his furie; which had hee knowne, hee had surely slaine her. *Iames* towne with her wild traine she as freely frequented, as her fathers habitation; and during the time of two or three yeeres, she next vnder God, was still the instrument to preserue this Colonie from death, famine and vtter confusion, which if in those times had once beene dissolued, *Virginia* might haue line as it was at our first arriuall to this day. Since then, this businesse hauing beene turned and varied by many accidents from that I left it at: it is most certaine, after a long and troublesome warre after my departure, betwixt her father and our Colonie, all which time shee was not heard of, about two yeeres after shee her selfe was taken prisoner, being so detained neere two yeeres longer, the Colonie by that meanes was relieued, peace concluded, and at last reiecting her barbarous condition, was maried to an *English* Gentleman, with whom at this present she is in England; the first Christian euer of that Nation, the first *Virginian* euer spake *English*, or had a childe in mariage by an *Englishman*, a matter surely, if my meaning bee truly considered and well vnderstood, worthy a Princes vnderstanding.

Thus most gracious Lady, I haue related to your Maiestie, what at your best leasure our approued Histories will account you at large, and done in the time of your Maiesties life, and howeuer this might bee presented you from a more worthy pen, it cannot from a more honest heart, as yet I neuer begged anything of the state, or any, and it is my want of abilitie and her exceeding desert, your birth, meanes and authorittie, hir birth, vertue, want and simplicitie, doth make mee thus bold, humbly to beseech your Maiestie to take this knowledge of her, though it be from one so vnworthy to be the reporter, as my selfe, her husbands estate not being able to make her fit to attend your Maiestie: the most and least I can doe, is to tell you this, because none so oft hath tried it as my selfe, and the rather being of so great a spirit, how euer her stature: if she should not be well receiued,

seeing this Kingdome may rightly haue a Kingdome by her meanes; her present loue to vs and Christianitie, might turne to such scorne and furie, as to diuert all this good to the worst of euill [evil], where finding so great a Queene should doe her some honour more than she can imagine, for being so kinde to your seruants and subiects, would so rauish her with content, as endeare her dearest bloud to effect that, your Maiestie and all the Kings honest subiects most earnestly desire: And so I humbly kisse your gracious hands.

Being about this time preparing to set saile for *New-England*, I could nor stay to doe her that seruice I desired, and she well deserued; but hearing shee was at *Branford* with diuers of my friends, I went to see her: After a modest salutation, without any word, she turned about, obscured her face, as not seeming well contented; and in that humour her husband, with diuers others, we all left her two or three houres, repenting my selfe to haue writ she could speake *English*. But not long after, she began to talke, and remembred mee well what courtesies shee had done: saying, You did promise *Powhatan* what was yours should bee his, and he the like to you; you called him father being in his land a stranger, and by the same reason so must I doe you: which though I would haue excused, I durst not allow of that title, because she was a Kings daughter; with a well set countenance she said, Were you not afraid to come into my fathers Countrie, and caused feare in him and all his people (but mee) and feare you here I should call you father; I tell you then I will, and you shall call mee childe, and so I will bee for euer and euer your Countrieman. They did tell vs alwaies you were dead, and I knew no other till I came to *Plimoth*; yet *Powhatan* did command *Vttamatomakkin* [Tomocomo] to seeke you, and know the truth, because your Countriemen will lie much.

This Saluage [Savage], one of *Powhatans* Councell, being amongst them held an vnderstanding fellow; the King purposely sent him, as they say, to number the people here, and informe him well what wee were and our state. Arriuing at Plimoth, according to his directions, he got a long sticke, whereon by notches hee did thinke to haue kept the number of all the men hee could see, but he was quickly wearie of that taske: Comming to *London*, where by chance I met him, hauing renewed our acquaintance, where many were desirous to heare and see his behauiour, hee rold me *Powhatan* did bid him to finde me out, to shew him our God, the King, Queene, and Prince, I so much had told them of: Concerning God, I told him the best I could, the King I heard he had seene, and the rest hee should see when he would; he denied euer to haue seene the King, till by circumstances he was satissied he had: Then he replyed very sadly, You gaue *Powhatan* a white Dog, which *Powhatan* fed as himselfe, but your King gaue me nothing, and I am better than your white Dog.

The small time I staid in *London*, diuers [diverse] Courtiers and others, my acquaintances, hath gone with mee to see her, that generally concluded, they did thinke God had a great hand in her conuersion,

and they haue seene many *English* Ladies worse fauoured, proportioned and behauioured, and as since I haue heard, it pleased both the King and Queenes Maiestie honourably to esteeme her; accompanied with that honourable Lady the Lady *De la Warre*, and that honourable Lord her husband, and diuers other persons of good qualities, both publikely at the maskes and otherwise, to her great satisfaction and content, which doubtlesse she would haue deserued, had she liued to arriue in *Virginia*.

DRAWING CONCLUSIONS:

1. How credible is this source?
2. Given that the status of the source is uncertain, how do you evaluate the historical value of this source?

CASE STUDY 2: WHAT WAS THE STRATEGY BEHIND THE 1622 POWHATAN SURPRISE ATTACK?

The surprise attack against the English in 1622, led by Powhatan's successor Opechancanough, cost the Virginia settlement dearly in lives. Fully one-quarter of the English population was killed in a single day, and famine increased the casualties over the subsequent year. Coincidentally, epidemic disease hit the English the following year, killing hundreds more people. For several years after 1622, the English struck a militantly defensive posture. Although they did not attempt to destroy the Powhatans altogether, they harassed them in an ongoing way while continuing to take up more land for cultivating tobacco. Opechancanough tried this same strategy again in 1644, launching another devastating surprise attack that once again failed to halt the colony's expansion. As can be seen in the scholarly arguments provided here and in the primary documents from this time period, the English response to these attacks seemed to make life even harder for the Powhatans. This fact raises important questions about Opechancanough's intentions. Did he hope to drive the English out of Tsenacommacah entirely, or was he simply continuing the containment policy established by Powhatan? Why, in either case, did his strategy fail to prevent the English from taking control over even more Powhatan lands?

GUIDING QUESTIONS:

1. What was Opechancanough's likely purpose in launching this attack?
2. How effective was this strategy for protecting the interests of the Powhatan people?

Source: J. Frederick Fausz, "Opechancanough: Indian Resistance Leader," in *Struggle and Survival in Colonial America,* edited by David G. Sweet and Gary B. Nash (Berkeley: University of California Press, 1981), 21–36.

3.1 J. FREDERICK FAUSZ, "OPECHANCANOUGH: INDIAN RESISTANCE LEADER" (1981)

Historian J. Frederick Fausz has written extensively on the history of Powhatan-English relations during the early seventeenth century. As you read his analysis of Opechancanough's historical significance, pay special attention to his interpretation regarding the differences between Opechancanough and Powhatan.

GUIDING QUESTION:

1. According to Fausz, what were the goals of the 1622 uprising led by Opechancanough?

In May 1607, as the loblolly pines swayed in the spring breeze and the sturgeon were beginning their spawning runs up the broad tidal rivers, a determined band of 105 Englishmen established an invasion beachhead among the fertile meadows and marshy lowlands of Indian Virginia. Only four decades later, with their once-meager numbers now swelled to some fifteen thousand persons, the invaders had made themselves the masters of tidewater Virginia.

The possessors of this rich land—the people the English defeated, displaced, and nearly annihilated in creating the first successful colony in British America—were Algonquian Indians, known collectively as the Powhatans. Because they lost and because historians of the United States have been the political descendants of the victorious English invaders, there have been few attempts to comprehend the personalities or motivations of the Virginia Indians. The legends and tales that abound about the romantic Pocahontas and her father the "Emperor" Powhatan, have remained popular primarily because they symbolize the so-called superiority and strength of the English conquerors. Pocahontas was a "good Indian" because she renounced her culture and

became a converted Englishwoman, while Powhatan confirmed the myths of Indian weakness by capitulating to the whites within a few years after 1607.

While it is true that Pocahontas and Powhatan dealt with the English presence as they saw fit, there was a more characteristic manner of responding to invaders in the context of Powhatan cultural traditions. This was the way represented by Opechancanough (O-puh-can-can-6), kinsman of Pocahontas and Powhatan and the much-vilified architect of the bloody Indian uprisings of 1622 and 1644.

Who was this man who has been referred to as the cruel leader of the "perfidious and inhumane" Powhatans, the "unflinching enemy . . . of the Saxon race," and a chieftain "of large Stature, noble Presence, and extraordinary Parts" who "was perfectly skill'd in the Art of Governing"?[1] Although few details are known about his early life or background, Opechancanough, or Mangopeesomon as he was later called by his people, was trained from boyhood to be a leader of the Powhatans in war and in peace.

When the English arrived in Virginia, they reported that Opechancanough was linked by blood and alliance to Powhatan, the supreme chieftain

---

1 Robert Beverley, *The History and Present State of Virginia (1705)*, ed. Louis B. Wright (Chapel Hill, N.C., 1947), 61; Edward Waterhouse, *A Declaration of the State of the Colony . . . and a Relation of the Barbarous Massacre* (London, 1622), p. 18; Henry R. Schoolcraft, *Archives of Aboriginal Knowledge* (Philadelphia, 1860), p. 98.

(Mamanatowick), who had constructed a proud and strong tidewater Indian empire in the last quarter of the sixteenth century. By 1607 Powhatan ruled the largest, most politically complex and culturally unified chiefdom in Virginia. Called Tsenacommacah (Sen-ah-comma-cah)—meaning "densely inhabited land"—this Indian chiefdom had a total population of some twelve thousand persons. Forged by conquest, based on efficient administration and common defense, and maintained by force of arms, tribute, religious beliefs, and the authoritarian personality of a determined ruler, Tsenacommacah was a sovereign and extensive political domain. Powhatan was regarded as the great lord of an integrated kinship society administered by carefully selected local chiefs, or governors, of much power and wealth. These tribal leaders were called *werowances* ("he who is rich"), and among them there was none stronger than Opechancanough. . . .

From a cluster of villages located near the present West Point, Virginia, where tributaries form the York River, Opechancanough ruled over the important Pamunkey tribe. The largest single tribe in Powhatan's domain, the Pamunkeys around 1607 had a population of some twelve hundred including over three hundred warriors. Their territory, called "Opechancheno" after their leader, abounded in fresh water, deer-filled forests, large villages, and acres of planted corn, tobacco, beans, and squash. The Pamunkeys' homeland was also rich in copper and in pearls from freshwater mussels, and Opechancanough's influence derived at least partially from his monopoly of the latter commodity.

The most important source of Opechancanough's power, and a significant factor in explaining many of his later actions, was undoubtedly his role as chief of the most fearsome band of Powhatan warriors. The English often spoke of how disciplined and fierce the Pamunkeys were and reported that Opechancanough was able to mobilize a thousand bowmen in two days' time. His warriors joined battle armed with skillfully made longbows, four-foot arrows, and wooden clubs; their faces and shoulders were smeared with scarlet pigment, and they were adorned with mussel shells, beads, copper medallions, feathers, bird talons, and fox fur.

Despite his considerable power and influence, in 1607 Opechancanough was still subordinate to Powhatan. Although second to his kinsman, Opitchapam, in the line of succession to the title of *Mama nato wick*, he was forced to do the great chief's bidding, just as was any other tribesman less endowed with talent and status. Powhatan had no rivals in tidewater Virginia. As long as he lived, all the *werowances*, including Opechancanough, owed him deference and paid him tribute from the tribes under their control.

In May 1607, only two weeks after the English landed at Jamestown, the *Mamanatowick* mobilized his *werowances* and decided to test the white men by force of arms. It was Opechancanough's duty to keep the more important English leaders distracted some miles upriver from the settlement while other *werowances* attacked James Fort. This assault by several hundred warriors failed to dislodge the English garrison, however, and within days Powhatan altered his strategy. He now decided to offer hospitality to the invaders, and again Opechancanough followed his lead by sending presents of food and overtures of peace to Jamestown.

Similarly, when in December 1607 the *Mamanatowick* desired his first audience with an Englishman, Opechancanough was dispatched to capture Captain John Smith, the most conspicuous leader at Jamestown, and to conduct him safely to Werowocomoco, Powhatan's capital. This Opechancanough did, although some of his own Pamunkey tribesmen called for the death of the white captain.

Opechancanough's inferior position was further emphasized in the February-March 1608 negotiations for a joint Anglo-Powhatan expedition against the Monacan Indians to the west. It was decided that Powhatan and Captain Christopher Newport, "being great Werowances" would not personally lead their forces into battle but would leave the military details to lesser war chiefs—John Smith and Opechancanough.[2]

---

2   Capt. John Smith, *A True Relation of . . . Virginia* (London, 1608), p. D3r-v.

Although there is no evidence that Opechancanough was ever disloyal to Powhatan in these years, he was an ambitious man who doubtless resented his subordinate status under the *Mamanatowick*. His position became increasingly undesirable after 1608, since while trying to preserve the tenuous peace advocated by Powhatan, he was forced to endure insufferable aggressions by the English. After September 1608 John Smith initiated a purposeful campaign of intimidation, using both threats and force to put Powhatan's people on the defensive. On one occasion Smith captured and imprisoned two Indian warriors, and Opechancanough was obliged to humble himself and negotiate for their release. He sent his own shooting glove and wrist guard to Smith as a token of goodwill and entreated the captain to free the hostages "for his sake."[3] The prisoners were eventually released, but the fact that Opechancanough had been forced to beg meant that the cost in pride had been high.

It was only a matter of time before the brash Smith took still further advantage of his reputed ability to intimidate Indian leaders. In January 1609 he brazenly led a contingent of armed Englishmen into Opechancanough's Pamunkey enclave in search of food. When the warriors refused to supply corn to the English, an enraged Smith grabbed Opechancanough by the hair and held a loaded pistol to his chest. He threatened the frightened *werowance* in front of the Pamunkeys and forced the tribesmen "to cast downe their armes little dreaming anie durst in that manner have used their king." Smith demanded pledges of good behavior and a regular corn tribute from Opechancanough's people and vowed to load his ship with their "dead carkasses" if they ever again crossed him. In addition, soon after this incident Smith physically assaulted a son of Opechancanough and "spurned [him] like a dogge."[4]

Such harsh and shockingly disrespectful treatment of a Pamunkey leader was unprecedented, and Opechancanough's credibility as a war chief and status as a "royal" *werowance* were jeopardized by such incidents. Perhaps as a result of this, sometime between 1608 and 1612 Opechancanough was humiliated by a fellow *werowance* named Pipsco. Pipsco brazenly stole away one of Opechancanough's favorite wives and flaunted his relationship with the woman for years afterward. In the light of such events, how was the Pamunkey chieftain to cope with his own declining status as well as with the larger threat that the increasingly aggressive English invaders posed to all of Indian Virginia?

Matters soon got worse for the Powhatans in general, although Opechancanough's particular position gradually improved after 1609. John Smith's policy of intimidation with limited bloodshed was succeeded in 1609 by a chaotic period during which short-sighted Englishmen senselessly robbed and murdered Indians. Violent retaliation by the Powhatans quickly escalated into full-scale warfare between 1609 and 1614. Although many Englishmen were killed at first, their overall position was eventually strengthened by increased financial and moral support from London, by large supplies of arms, and by the arrival in Virginia of several dozen fighting men under experienced military commanders.

This First Anglo-Powhatan War proved disastrous for the Powhatans. In a series of sharp and brutal engagements, armored English musketeers attacked tribe after tribe until they gained control of the James River from Chesapeake Bay to the fall line. Powhatan, the aging chief, was unable to halt the English advance, but Opechancanough and his Pamunkeys fared better. In November 1609 they decimated an English force that had come to steal corn, and the result was that the leaders of the colony cautiously waited until 1613 before they felt confident enough to invade the Pamunkeys' territory again. Because of their strength in arms and the placement of their villages at some distance from the area of most active fighting along the James River, the Pamunkeys were spared the worst ravages of the war. Relative to

---

3 *Ibid.*, p. E3v.

4 [William Symonds, comp.], *The Proceedings of the English Colonie in Virginia since their first beginning . . . till this present 1612* (Oxford, 1612), pp. 69, 74.

Powhatan's declining power and the losses sustained by other area tribes, the Pamunkeys under Opechancanough became ever stronger.

Powhatan, the once-awesome ruler of tidewater Virginia, spent the war years largely in seclusion. The repeated English onslaughts had taken their toll on the energy and abilities of the *Mamanatowick*, already in his late sixties. By this time Powhatan "delighted in security, and pleasure, and . . . peace," and desired to be "quietly settled amongst his owne." He had tired of conflict. "I am old," he told the English, "and ere long must die . . . I knowe it is better to eat good meat, lie well, and sleep with my women and children, laugh and be merrie . . . then [to] bee forced to flie . . . and be hunted."[5] Powhatan's favorite daughter, Pocahontas, was captured by the English in 1613. In the next year she renounced her heritage, accepted the Anglican faith, and prepared to marry an English planter, John Rolfe. But Powhatan stubbornly refused to capitulate to the English until the Pamunkeys under Opechancanough were attacked by a large force of armed musketeers. Now a broken man, Powhatan meekly accepted a humiliating peace treaty in the spring of 1614. He who might have crushed the English in 1607 found himself, only seven years later, pathetically entreating his enemies for a shaving knife, bone combs, fishhooks, and a dog and cat.

While Powhatan contented himself with making ceremonial tours throughout his domain after 1614, Opechancanough boldly stepped into the power vacuum created by the war. In the year of the peace, Indian informants told colony leaders that whatever Opechancanough "agreed upon and did, the great King [Powhatan] would confirme." The English noted that Opechancanough was the Powhatans' "chief Captaine, and one that can as soone (if not sooner) as Powhatan commande the men." And in 1615 it was reported that Opechancanough "hath

already the commaund of all the people." Finally in the summer of 1617, Powhatan, grief-stricken upon learning of Pocahontas's death in England, allegedly "left the Government of his Kingdom to Opachanko [Opechancanough] and his other brother [Opitchapam]" and sought refuge among the Patawomeke tribe along the Potomac River.[6]

Powhatan's abdication in 1617 revealed a power struggle among the tidewater Indian *werowances*. At the center of this contest was Opechancanough, who deftly used the English to increase his authority over the area tribes. In 1616 he convinced the proud and quick-tempered governor of the colony, George Yeardley, that the independent Chickahominy tribe had been killing English livestock. This carefully planted information resulted in an English attack during which some forty Chickahominies were treacherously murdered. It was no coincidence that Opechancanough was nearby to witness the slaughter and that he quickly stepped forward to comfort the bloodied and frightened Chickahominies. That tribe then declared Opechancanough their king, gave him their allegiance, and agreed to pay him tribute. As John Smith later explained these events, Opechancanough had succeeded in his plan "for the subjecting of those people, that neither hee nor Powhatan could ever [before] bring to their obedience."[7]

Such maneuvers clearly demonstrated Opechancanough's ambition; and upon Powhatan's death in April 1618 the wily Pamunkey *werowance* became the effective overlord of the tidewater tribes. Opechancanough was finally the "great Kinge," and as "a great Captaine" who "did always fight," he was called upon to use his talents and status in an active, dangerous struggle against the English. But his lust for political control was not only a personal one; it was also an unselfish and desperate attempt to prevent the total collapse of a weakened and threatened

---

5   *Ibid.*, pp. 60–61.
6   Ralph Hamor, *A True Discourse of the Present Estate of Virginia . . . till . . . 1614* (London, 1615), pp. 10, 53; Capt. Samuel Argall to Virginia Company of London, March 10, 1617/18, and to Council for Virginia, June 9, 1617, in Susan Myra Kingsbury, ed., *Records of the Virginia Company of London*, 4 vols. (Washington, D.C., 1906–35, vol. 3, pp. 73–74, 92.
7   Capt. John Smith, *The Generall Historie of Virginia, New-England, and the Summer Isles* (London, 1624), p. 120.

Tsenacommacah. Between 1618 and 1622, Opechancanough's priorities were clearly focused on strengthening and revitalizing his people.

The challenges he faced were immense. In the years immediately following the First Anglo-Powhatan War, the English had dispossessed the Indians of much of their best land. This was especially true after 1618, when a boom in tobacco prices sharpened English land appetites, and famine and disease wracked the once-strong Powhatans. Poor harvests made the Indians dependent on their hated enemies for food, while epidemics devastated the Powhatans and even the deer in their forests between 1617 and 1619. Although disease attacked all the tidewater tribes, Opechancanough's Pamunkeys may have suffered proportionately less than other Powhatans because their territory lay at some distance from the English settlements.

In the wake of these tragedies the Powhatans were pitiable but not pitied. Their English enemies regarded the debilitated, depopulated, and seemingly unthreatening Indians more as defeated and downtrodden pawns than as proud and fierce warriors. Complacent in the peace of 1614 and temporarily less dependent on the Indians for food, the English considered the Powhatans merely impotent and troublesome obstacles to the exploitation of Virginia's lands and resources. It was in these exceedingly adverse circumstances that Opechancanough began his methodical consolidation of the remnants of Powhatan's once-united chiefdom, along with the recruitment of tribes like the Chickahominies who had never been a part of Tsenacommacah. It was ironic that although Opechancanough had often displayed his potential for leadership, it was only the harsh presence of the English that brought him to the fore.

Opechancanough's plan depended on manipulating two intertwined social pressures: the desire of the Indians to procure the colonists' muskets and the attempts of the English to convert and "civilize" the Powhatans. The Virginia Company of London, the joint-stock corporation in charge of colony affairs, was sincerely interested in Christianizing and educating Indian youths, and colonial officials approached Opechancanough many times in an effort to borrow or even buy Powhatan children for this purpose. But the chief refused to allow any Indians to live among the English unless they were permitted the use of muskets. Ever since 1607 the Powhatans had been attempting to obtain firearms from the English. Recognizing that this single technological advantage was the key to English domination, Opechancanough was determined somehow to alter the colonists' monopoly of muskets. Faced with his refusal to provide children for Christianization and under unceasing pressure from missionary idealists among the company's investors in London, the Virginia leaders finally allowed some Powhatans to be trained in the use of firearms.

Thus, while the colonists were preoccupied with growing tobacco and were complacent about the Indians' reputed powerlessness, Opechancanough's men were becoming competent marksmen. By 1618 Englishmen were occasionally being killed by Indians using muskets, and it was reported that the Powhatans would be "boulde . . . to assault" white settlements whenever they concluded that English firearms were "sicke and not to be used" against them.[8]

By 1622 Opechancanough's leadership had made the tidewater tribes stronger than at any other time since 1607. The English judged the chief's own stronghold so defensible that three hundred musketeers—more men than had been drawn together in a single force during the First Anglo-Powhatan War—would be required to launch an attack against the Pamunkeys. This was a far cry from the English assessment of a decade before that the Indians were incapable of inflicting harm.

Opechancanough had succeeded in engineering this military renaissance and the psychological revitalization of his people in large part through the efforts of Nemattanew (Nemát-ten-yū) a mysterious prophet, war captain, and advisor, who was himself one of the first Powhatans to become an able marksman with English muskets. Called "Jack of

---

8   *Ibid.*, p. 125; H. R. McIlwaine, ed., *Journals of the House of Burgesses of Virginia, 1619–1658/59* (Richmond, 1915), pp. 33–34.

the Feathers" by the colonists, Nemattanew always went about attired in elaborate and unique feather garments, "as thowghe he meant to flye." He was respected by the Powhatans, and by Opechancanough especially, as a charismatic and talented policymaker, while the English called him a "very cunning fellow" who "took great Pride in preserving and increasing . . . [the Indians'] Superstition concerning him, affecting every thing that was odd and prodigious to work upon their Admiration." Significantly, Nemattanew told his people that he was immortal, that he was therefore invulnerable to English bullets, and that he possessed "an Ointment" and special powers "that could secure them" from bullets as well.[9]

By the spring of 1621, as Nemattanew's revitalizing influence grew among the Powhatans, Opechancanough made plans to annihilate the hated English. His first step was to conclude a firm peace with the colony so that the whites would confidently put aside their muskets for plows and allow the Powhatans to move freely among their plantations. Then, further to lure the English into complacency, Opechancanough decided to tell his adversaries what they wanted to hear concerning the religious and cultural conversion of his people.

He was able to accomplish his goals because in 1620–21 the Virginia Company had sent two naive and optimistic reformers to the colony to implement its program for the "civilization" of the Indians. These men were Sir Francis Wyatt, Jamestown's new governor, and George Thorpe, an idealistic proselytizer. They tried to win over Opechancanough's people with lavish gifts, English clothes, and kind words. Wyatt and especially Thorpe set out to undermine Powhatan religion and traditions and to alienate Indian youths from their elders by promoting English customs and Christianity among them. This energetic new campaign seemed especially dangerous to Opechancanough; but he acted coolly and resourcefully in the face of it.

Late in 1621 Opechancanough met with the zealous Thorpe, who had been trying to convert him

for months, and to the astonishment of everyone renounced the major teachings of Powhatan religion. He promised to allow English families to live among the Pamunkeys and gave his permission for the colonists to take any lands not actually occupied by the Powhatans! These startling announcements would have amounted to heresy had they been made sincerely, but Opechancanough was purposefully deceptive in initiating the final chapter in his consolidation of power. By lulling Thorpe, Wyatt, and the other Englishmen into complacency, Opechancanough was forging a strategy more subtle in its execution, more ethnocentric in its foundation, and more revolutionary in its potential impact than Thorpe's.

Thanks to the efforts of Opechancanough and Nemattanew, the Powhatans were by this time more strongly committed to their own culture than ever. Opechancanough saw clearly that there could be no Anglo-Powhatan relations based on peace. Every tragedy that could have befallen the Indians had occurred, and the English had brought destruction to the tribes as readily in times of peace as in times of war. A prolonged peace could only result in more seizures of Indian corn and territory and in further attempts to destroy his people's culture. What did the Powhatans have to gain by keeping the peace? What could they lose by breaking it?

From Opechancanough's personal standpoint, everything the English had done before 1621 had served to increase his power and leverage in Powhatan politics; anything they might do from that time forward was likely to weaken his position. The chief's bold strategy with Thorpe nevertheless revealed confidence in the Indians' future rather than despair. Opechancanough had no intention of leading the Powhatans into physical or cultural suicide; his statements and actions reflected strength and pride, not weakness or desperation.

Opechancanough's plans were suddenly put in jeopardy when in early March 1622 some Englishmen "accidentally" murdered the "immortal"

---

9   George Percy, "A Trewe Relacyon . . . of Virginia from . . . 1609 untill . . . 1612," in *Tyler's Quarterly Historical and Genealogical Magazine* 3 (1922): 280; Beverley, *History*, pp. 52–53; Smith, *Generall Historie of Virginia*, pp. 144, 151; J. Frederick Fausz and Jon Kukla, "A Letter of Advice to the Governor of Virginia, 1624," *William and Mary Quarterly* 34 (1977): 117.

Nemattanew under suspicious circumstances. But Powhatan resiliency and Opechancanough's resolve were confirmed only two weeks later when, as spring breezes once again replaced winter's chill among the pines, an impressive Indian alliance suddenly attacked the English settlements along the entire length of the James River. In this famous uprising of March 22, 1622, Opechancanough's warriors infiltrated white homesteads without arousing suspicion and managed to kill some 330 people before the colony mobilized its forces. Shocked and frightened by this bold and bloody stroke, the English grudgingly recognized Opechancanough's skill as the "Great generall of the Salvages."[10]

The 1622 uprising touched off a ten-year war, and for a brief time Powhatan warriors outdid their enemies, using muskets made in England. Distraught whites reported that the Indians became "verie bold, and can use peeces [muskets] . . . as well or better than an Englishman." With the Powhatans well armed with captured weapons, the colonists feared that they would "brave our countrymen at their verie doors."[11]

This Second Anglo-Powhatan War reached its peak in autumn 1624, when an intertribal force of eight hundred warriors, dominated by Pamunkeys, fought English musketeers in a fierce, two-day battle in open field. In this unusual engagement waged in Pamunkey territory, Opechancanough's warriors fought to defend their homeland and to preserve their excellent reputation among other area tribes. Although the Pamunkeys were eventually forced to retreat, never before had the Indians demonstrated such tenacity under fire. Even Governor Wyatt had to admit that this battle "shewed what the Indyans could doe."[12]

Recognizing Openchancanough's importance to the Indians' courage and persistence, Jamestown officials placed a bounty on his head. The English came close to killing him in 1623 by means of an elaborate plot to ambush and poison several parleying chiefs. Opechancanough was almost certainly present at the meeting, where many Indian leaders died, but somehow he managed to escape the English trap.

The war continued, but by 1625 both sides had come to the realization that the annihilation of their enemies was impossible. For almost three years Governor Wyatt and his commanders had "used their uttermost and Christian endeavours in prosecutinge revenge against the bloody Salvadges" without making Opechancanough or his people submit. The Pamunkey *werowance* had proved a better "generall" than Powhatan, and in 1625 the fatigued English soldiers decided to suspend their twice-yearly campaigns against him. Choosing to plant tobacco rather than to pursue the utter destruction of the Powhatans, the colonists had, in Governor Wyatt's words, "worne owt the Skarrs of the Massacre."[13]

Although the Second Anglo-Powhatan War did not end officially until 1632, the early years of the conflict were the most significant in demonstrating that the Indians' pride had not been extinguished by a decade and a half of disruptive and frequently brutal contact with the Englishmen. By war's end it might be said that Opechancanough had won a qualified victory. If he had not succeeded in annihilating the colonists, he had at least ended the threat of enforced culture change. His people had willingly risked death rather than adopt the Christian religion and English manners. Although many Powhatans did die, their traditions were for the time being preserved.

After peace was agreed to in 1632, there followed a decade of tenuous coexistence between the Powhatans and the English. The Indians had been weakened by the war, and they welcomed an opportunity to

---

10   [Anon.], "Good Newes from Virginia" (broadside ballad, ca. 1622–23), in *William and Mary Quarterly* 5 (1948): 354.

11   Richard Frethorne to his parents, April 3, 1623, in Kingsbury, *Records*, vol. 4, p. 61; Report on conditions in Virginia, May 1623, *ibid.*, p. 147.

12   Sir Francis Wyatt to the Earl of Southampton and the Virginia Company, December 2, 1624, *ibid.*, pp. 507–508.

13   *Ibid.* [Kingsbury, *Records*, vol. 4, 507–508]; Governor Wyatt to commissioners investigating Virginia, January 4, 1625/26, *ibid.*, pp. 568–569.

tend their fields in peace. In the long run, however, the period after 1632 proved more damaging to the Powhatans than the war years. The Virginia colony developed so rapidly that the Indians' territorial and cultural foundations were quickly and irrevocably eroded. After a dozen years, with nowhere to go and with a smaller and smaller amount of land on which to preserve their traditions and to raise their children, the Powhatans once again chose the desperate option of war.

In the spring of 1644, as the sturgeon and the meadows again experienced nature's season of renewal, the tireless Opechancanough mobilized a new generation of warriors for an even more desperate rebellion. As in 1622, the Powhatans struck at the English plantations without warning and killed some five hundred of the land-hungry colonists. But this uprising proved futile, for by this time the odds against success were overwhelming. In 1646, after almost two years of brutal warfare, the by now infirm but indefatigable Pamunkey chief, who had seen some eighty winters, was captured and murdered by the English.

Opechancanough's death ended a talented and tempestuous career of leadership that spanned four eventful decades. He had known and warred with an entire generation of Englishmen, long since dead. The Virginia governor who captured him in 1646 had been a mere babe in the cradle when Jamestown was founded.

The last of the "true" Powhatans, Opechancanough had symbolized the precontact glory of Tsenacommacah, while adapting to the postcontact exigencies of cultural survival. He had demonstrated resiliency and political resolve in his magnificent effort to save the Powhatan way of life, and he had in fact succeeded in the difficult task of rebuilding and enlarging Powhatan's domain after the first peace with the English in 1614. The Pamunkeys' resort to arms in two bloody wars between 1622 and 1646 reveal that Opechancanough had managed to reinstill pride and purpose in his people.

Opechancanough coped as best he knew how with the strange and aggressive forces of European colonization. Although his indomitable courage and unyielding fight against foreign domination failed to prevent the eventual subjugation of the Powhatans, Opechancanough's refusal to submit was a reassertion of the proud warrior traditions of his culture. He led his people in a struggle for survival while trying to preserve their self-respect. When the Powhatans had to choose between cultural survival and individual sacrifice, they proudly chose death over enslavement. Victory or defeat mattered less to them than the act of resistance.

In this the "Great generall" set a strong personal example. Even as a captive in 1646, the exhausted Opechancanough displayed pride and dignity until the end. Just before he was treacherously shot in the back by an English guard, the aged Pamunkey *werowance*—"so decrepit that he was not able to walk alone," with "Eye-lids . . . so heavy that he could not see"—was protesting the fact that he had been placed on public exhibition like a caged animal.[14] For such a man and such a culture in such an era, the ability to cope was the ability to fight bravely against overwhelming odds and to die with dignity and purpose.

DRAWING CONCLUSIONS:

1. How does Fausz evaluate the consequences of Opechancanough's strategies for responding to English expansionism?

---

14 Beverley, *History,* p. 62.

3.2 FREDERIC W. GLEACH, "'THE GREAT MASSACRE OF 1622'" (1997)

Historical anthropologist Frederic Gleach has attempted to root his study of the English conquest of Tsenacommacah in a deep understanding of the Powhatan worldview and motives. In this excerpt, he applies this approach to the Powhatan surprise attack against the English in 1622. Note that the title of this excerpt is itself a quotation, as the English usually referred to this event as a "Great Massacre." Gleach does not necessarily endorse this view of the event, as he is well aware of the dire circumstances within which the Powhatans found themselves, and he makes the case here that their motives were complex.

GUIDING QUESTION:

1. How does Gleach interpret the intentions behind the 1622 attack?

"'THE GREAT MASSACRE OF 1622'"

In early 1622 the great warrior Nemattanew was killed by the English.[15] According to the historical accounts, he went to the private settlement of an Englishman named Morgan and persuaded him to go to Pamunkey to exchange some goods he had that Nemattanew wanted. This Morgan was never again heard from. Within a few days, Nemattanew returned to Morgan's house, where he met two young men, servants, who asked after Morgan. Nemattanew was wearing Morgan's cap, which the boys recognized, and he told them Morgan was dead. The two tried to take Nemattanew to the authorities: "But he refused to go, and very insolently abused them. Whereupon they shot him down, and as they were carrying him to the governor, he died" (Beverley 1947:53). This governor was Sir Francis

---

Excerpt from Frederic W. Gleach, "'The Great Massacre of 1622,'" in *Powhatan's World and Colonial Virginia: A Conflict of Cultures* (Lincoln: University of Nebraska Press, 1997), 148–158.

15 Browne's entry for the month of March in his 1622 almanac was oddly prophetic for the Virginia colony: the "phlebotomy" skillfully applied by the Powhatans that month, the coup of 22 March, proved to be truly dangerous medicine for the physician, since the English colony took this as stimulant to a war of revenge. Rountree (1990:71–72) has suggested that Nemattanew's killing occurred prior to November 1621, but, as she notes, all contemporary accounts that mention the timing of these events "indicate a short lapse of time between his death and the attack" (1990:302 n.44). She bases her timing on an inferred sequence of events from a confusingly written passage in a letter from the Virginia Council (Rountree 1990:302 n.45). The critical statement reads, "neither was it to be imagined that upon the death of Nemattanew, a man so far out of the favor of Opechancanough that he sent word to Sir George Yeardley being then governor by his interpreter, that for his part he could be contented his throat were cut, there would fall out a general breach" (Virginia Council 1935: 10–11). The mention of Yeardley as governor places the cited message from Opechancanough prior to Wyatt's arrival in November 1621, but there is no reason that a character reference in a subordinate clause need refer to action precisely contemporary with the main text in which the clause is embedded. The primary text should be read thus: "Neither was it to be imagined that upon the death of Nemattanew there would fall out a general breach." The subordinate clause indicates why this should be so: prior to November 1621 some incident had prompted a message to the governor that Nemattanew was so out of favor that Opechancanough could be contented if Nemattanew's throat were cut. From this I assume that Nemattanew had raided other settlements. The statement is clearly not relevant to the immediate time of Nemattanew's death, since he died of gunshot wounds before he could be taken to the governor (Beverley 1947:53).

Wyatt, who had replaced Yeardley in November 1621. As Nemattanew was dying, he asked the boys not to tell how he was killed; he also asked to be buried among the English. The English viewed this event as the cause of the 1622 coup (Beverley 1947:53).

When Opechancanough received word of this murder, he reputedly "much grieved and repined, with great threats of revenge; but the English returned him such terrible answers, that he cunningly dissembled his intent, with the greatest signs he could of love and peace" (Smith 1986:293). On 22 March 1622, less than two weeks after Nemattanew's death (Smith 1986:293), the coup took place (Beverley 1947:51–55; Virginia Council 1933:612; Waterhouse 1933:550–56). That morning the Indians went into the English settlements, even using their boats to cross the rivers, as had become usual. Presents of food had been taken the previous evening, and on that morning some joined the colonists in their breakfasts, and worked alongside them in the fields. Having entered the settlements unarmed, when the time came they picked up the colonists' tools and weapons and killed them all, men, women, and children, old and young alike, "so sudden in their cruel execution that few or none discerned the weapon or blow that brought them to destruction" (Waterhouse 1933:551). The bodies of some of the slain were also mutilated. This attack fell as a single stroke across much of the colony, without successive attacks: "whatever was not done by surprise that day, was left undone, and many that made early resistance escaped" (Beverley 1947:51). According to the official counts, 347 colonists were killed; a "true list of the names of all those that were massacred" was included in the printed account by Waterhouse (1933:564–71), but there were no reports from some settlements, such as Bermuda Hundred, so the total number killed could have been higher. After its dissolution, the Virginia Company stated that "about 400 of our people were slain" in this attack (Virginia Co. 1935:524). Many isolated settlements, decreased in size by the company policy of concentrating population in Jamestown, were completely wiped out. At the Falling Creek ironworks, for example, "no soul was saved, but a boy and a girl, who, with great difficulty, hid themselves" (Beverley 1947:55).

Some settlements, on the other hand, emerged unscathed, either fighting off the attackers or not being attacked in the first place [Map 4]. According to tradition, Jamestown was saved by a warning from a Christianized Indian boy named Chanco, but there is no first- or even secondhand account of an attack taking place there. One would expect to have descriptions of the successful defense against the Indians, if such occurred, particularly since accounts of other such defenses are given.

. . .

As at Jamestown, there was no attack recorded in the Corporation of Elizabeth City, at the mouth of the James River. The Indians of this area were among those only recently conquered by the Powhatans, and it has traditionally been assumed that they simply did not go along with the coup (e.g., Fausz 1977:399). The distribution of attacks can be interpreted in that way; many more attacks occurred west of Jamestown than to the east, which reflects the historical orientation of Powhatan control. It could also reflect the intentions of the Powhatans, however. In those areas attacked, not only were the colonists killed, but scalping and other acts of degradation were also committed:

> not being content with taking away life alone, they fell after again upon the dead, making as well as they could a fresh murder, defacing, dragging, and mangling the dead carcasses into many pieces, and carrying some parts away in derision, with base and brutish triumph. (Waterhouse 1933:551)
>
> Captain Nathaniel Powell, another of the council, who had some time been governor of the country, was also killed. He was one of the first planters, a brave soldier, had deserved well in all ways, was universally valued and esteemed by all parties and factions and none in the country better known among the Indians. Yet they slew both him and his family, and afterwards haggled their bodies, and cut off his head, to express their utmost height of scorn and cruelty. (Smith 1865:212)

Given the Powhatans' aesthetic of war, an attitude of "derision" or "scorn" is probably a reasonably accurate partial description; the point in acts such as these was to humiliate the defeated opponent, to demonstrate his relative weakness. But at the same time, if he was a worthy individual his strength was desired. Either way, the application of skill, shrewdness, and wit were of utmost importance. George Thorpe seems to have received particular attention: "And both [Opechancanough] and his people for the daily courtesies this good gentleman did to one or another of them, did profess such outward love and respect unto him, as nothing could seem more; but all was little regarded after by this viperous brood, as the sequel showed: for they not only willfully murdered him, but cruelly and fiercely, out of devilish malice, did so many barbarous despites and foul scorns after to his dead corpse, as are unbefitting to be heard by any civil ear" (Waterhouse 1933:552–53). Thorpe's estate would later suffer abuses at the hands of his fellow Englishmen, who were simply exercising greed; these "barbarous despites and foul scorns" inflicted by the Powhatans probably demonstrated an element of respect for Thorpe as an individual, as well as derision of the English and their culture.

By means of such acts the attackers demonstrated their superiority from the Powhatan perspective. The English reaction, however, was just the opposite: "these miscreants, contrariwise in this kind, not only put off humanity, but put on a worse and more than unnatural brutishness" (Waterhouse 1933:551). The Powhatans reduced themselves to a state below that of wild beasts, in the colonists' perception. Although there would be calls from England to continue the attempts to convert them, the English colonists in Virginia would pursue a harsh policy of aggression: "Because the way of conquering them is much more easy than of civilizing them by fair means, for they are a rude, barbarous, and naked people, scattered in small companies, which are helps to victory, but hinderances to civility" (Waterhouse 1933:557). The English perceived the Powhatans as defeated, but the Powhatans themselves consistently acted to maintain their position of superiority in the relationship, and they clearly saw themselves as dominating the English. This is evident from their exchanges, beginning with those between Powhatan and Captain John Smith, and up to and including the coup itself. The Powhatans had absorbed the English into their own culture, although the English refused to see it that way.

This coup has been interpreted by Fausz (1977:345–49) as an "uprising," founded in a revitalization movement which had Nemattanew as its leader—after only fifteen years of interaction. The killing of Nemattanew then produced a state of "desperation" in Opechancanough (Fausz 1977:356) and prompted him to attack immediately. The political and social reasons why this should not be viewed as an uprising have already been noted; there is also another misunderstanding of Powhatan world-view involved in such a characterization.

. . .

The coup had probably been in planning since at least the previous year, when Opechancanough and Itoyatan took on new names, reflecting new positions or status; Rountree (1990:66–73) believes that it had been in planning for several years. The murder of Nemattanew was supposed the proximate cause of it, although the English recognized another long-term factor: "that in time we by our growing continually upon them, would dispossess them of this country" (Waterhouse 1933:556). The English, who had originally informed Powhatan that they intended to stay only long enough to repair their boat (Smith 1986a:54–55), and who had twice been offered their own lands in which to live in peace, continued to take over lands beyond what was offered, often killing the inhabitants to do so. Such a killing by an inferior generally had to be revenged, or paid off, within the Powhatan culture (cf. Warren 1984:198), although the *Mamanatowick* could excuse a killing, in effect accepting the responsibility for the act. Nemattanew was an important war-chief, but as Opechancanough had assured the English the previous year, the death of "but one man should be no occasion for the breach of the peace" (Virginia Council 1935:11). A single murder might need to be revenged, but it need not start a war.

The killing of Nemattanew was thus but one element in determining the attack against the English. Even before that event, the coup was probably planned for this time of year. Food supplies for the English and the Powhatans alike were at their shortest in the late winter and early spring, but whereas the English repeatedly had to rely on food obtained from the Powhatans to get through the winter, Smith had noted in January 1608 "the plenty he had seen, especially at Werowocomoco, and . . . the state and bounty of Powhatan (which till that time was unknown)" (Smith 1986:152). The assumption by the English of barely adequate stores for the Powhatans was more likely a projection of their own situation. The English would thus be at their weakest at this time and in a worse position than the Powhatans. The timing is also strikingly close to the quarter moon, which, according to an English almanac for that year, was on 23 March (Browne 1622:n.p.); the lunar quarters were a time marker of native significance, as recorded for the neighboring Delaware Indians: "They distinguish the phases of the moon by particular names; they say the 'new moon,' the 'round moon' (when it is full), and when in its decline, they say it is 'half round'" (Heckewelder 1876:308). Furthermore, the Indians, including Opechancanough, were probably aware that this was a holy season for the English, falling between Ash Wednesday and Easter. This assertion is based on the fact that George Thorpe often conferred with Opechancanough "and intimated to him matters of our religion" (Waterhouse 1933:552). This would give the sacrifice of the English colonists an ironic religious overtone as a physical instantiation of their rejection of the English Church as it was being forced on them.

Fausz (1977:359–60) suggested that this was a dangerous time for the Powhatans to go to war, because "in March . . . the Powhatan economy afforded little or no corn surplus from the previous autumn's harvests, and planting for the next season would not begin until late April." As already suggested, this was a misperception, and the Powhatans' ability to survive later colonial attempts to starve them out reinforces my previous observations. The question is moot, however, since food supplies were not critical for the Powhatans: they were not planning an extended campaign. This was to be a coup, not a protracted war. The Indians suffered no significant losses during the attack—and yet they did not continue beyond that single simultaneous stroke across the colony. There was no further assault on the colonists until 9 September 1622, when four laborers were reportedly killed (Smith 1986:312).

The destruction could have been much greater—if that had been the plan. Contrary to the English perception, however, this was plainly no attempt at extermination. Neither was it intended to drive the colonists back to England, as Rountree (1990:75) suggests; the colonists were valued for the material goods they could provide, as the original negotiations between Smith and Powhatan made clear. But they were unruly; they refused to live as they were supposed to. When viewed from the perspective of the history of interactions, when considered in the context of traditional native forms of war, and when taken into consideration with other aspects of the attack, it seems clear that the Powhatans' goal was not to remove the English but rather to confine them in a small territory, put a halt to their local Christianization efforts, and demonstrate the Powhatans' superiority over the English. The warning of the colonists near Jamestown, seen in this light, was but one step toward that goal: the desired result was to get the settlers to remove from their scattered, indefensible settlements to the comparative safety of Jamestown—and thus to return them to a single location, in which they could be more closely controlled. Farther outlying settlements were destroyed to ensure they would not be reoccupied and to make clear that such settlements were inappropriate for the English colonists. This coup was intended to be "a bold and effective strike, which would long be remembered, and keep their enemies in fear and check" (Warren 1984:127, writing on Ojibwa warfare).

BIBLIOGRAPHY

Robert Beverley, *The History and Present State of Virginia* [1705], edited by Louis B. Wright. (Chapel Hill: University of North Carolina Press, 1947).

Daniel Browne, *A New Almanacke and Prognostication for the Yeare of Our Lord God, 1622* (London, 1622).

J. Frederick Fausz, *The Powhatan Uprising of 1622: A Historical Study of Ethnocentrism and Cultural Conflict* (PhD dissertation: College of William and Mary, 1977).

John Heckewelder, *History, Manners, and Customs of the Indian Nations Who Once Inhabited Pennsylvania and the Neighboring States* (Philadelphia: Historical Society of Pennsylvania, 1876).

Helen C. Rountree, *Pocahontas's People: The Powhatan Indians of Virginia through Four Centuries* (Norman: Univ. of Oklahoma Press, 1990).

John Smith, *The Generall Historie of Virginia, New-England, and the Summer Isles* [1624], in *The Complete Works of Captain John Smith (1580 1631)*, edited by Philip L. Barbour (Chapel Hill, University of North Carolina Press, 1986).

William Smith, *The History of the First Discovery and Settlement of Virginia* [1747] (New York: Reprinted for Joseph Sabin, 1865).

Virginia Company of London, "Discourse of the Old Company" [April 1625], in *The Records of the Virginia Company of London*, Vol. 4, edited by Susan M. Kingsbury (Washington, DC: U.S. Government Printing Office, 1935).

Virginia Council, "A Letter to the Virginia Company of London" [(after 20) April 1622], in *The Records of the Virginia Company of London*, Vol. 3, edited by Susan M. Kingsbury (Washington, DC: U.S. Government Printing Office, 1933).

———, "Letter to Virginia Company of London," [20 January 1623], in *The Records of the Virginia Company of London*, Vol. 4, edited by Susan M. Kingsbury (Washington, DC: U.S. Government Printing Office, 1935).

William W. Warren, *A History of the Ojibway People* [1885] (Saint Paul: Minnesota Historical Society Press, 1984).

Edward Waterhouse, *A Declaration of the State of the Colony and Affaires in Virginia* [1622], in *Records of the Virginia Company of London*, Vol. 3, edited by Susan M. Kingsbury (Washington DC: US Government Printing Office, 1933).

DRAWING CONCLUSIONS:

1. How does Gleach's interpretation of the 1622 "coup" differ from that of Fausz? How do you explain this difference in perspective?

2. How does your understanding of the 1622 attack help you respond to the Big Question about how the English were able to seize the lands of the Powhatan people?

ADDITIONAL RESOURCES

BOOKS & ARTICLES

Billings, Warren M. *The Old Dominion in the Seventeenth Century: A Documentary History of Virginia, 1606-1700*. Rev. edition. Chapel Hill: University of North Carolina Press, 2007.

Brown, Kathleen, M. *Good Wives, Nasty Wenches, and Anxious Patriarchs: Gender, Race, and Power in Colonial Virginia*. Chapel Hill: University of North Carolina Press, 1996.

Gleach, Frederic W. *Powhatan's World and Colonial Virginia: A Conflict of Cultures*. Lincoln: University of Nebraska Press, 1997.

Kupperman, Karen O. *The Jamestown Project*. Cambridge, MA: Harvard University Press, 2007.

Lemay, A. Leo. *Did Pocahontas Save Captain John Smith?* Athens: University of Georgia Press, 1992.

Linwood, Custalow and Angela L. Daniel. *The True Story of Pocahontas: The Other Side of History*. Golden, CO: Fulcrum Publishing, 2007.

Mancall, Peter C. *Envisioning America: English Plans for the Colonization of North America, 1580-1640*. New York: Bedford/St. Martin's, 1995.

Morgan, Edmund, S. *American Slavery, American Freedom*. Reissue ed. New York: W. W. Norton & Company, 2003.

Richter, Daniel, K. *Before the Revolution: America's Ancient Pasts*. Cambridge, MA: Harvard University Press, 2011.

Richter, Daniel, K. *Facing East from Indian Country: A Native History of Early America*. Cambridge, MA: Harvard University Press, 2003.

Rountree, Helen, C. *Pocahontas, Powhatan, Opechancanough: Three Indian Lives Changed by Jamestown*. Charlottesville: University of Virginia Press, 2006.

Rountree, Helen, C. *Pocahontas's People: The Powhatan Indians of Virginia Through Four Centuries*. Norman: University of Oklahoma Press, 1990.

Rountree, Helen, C. *Powhatan Foreign Relations, 1500-1722*. Charlottesville: University of Virginia Press, 1993.

Schmidt, Ethan A. "Cockacoeske, Weroansqua of the Pamunkeys, and Indian Resistance in Seventeenth-Century Virginia." *American Indian Quarterly* 36 (Summer 2012): 288–317.

Smith, John. *Captain John Smith: Writings with Other Narratives of Roanoke, Jamestown, and the First English Settlement of America*. Edited by James Horn. New York: Library of America, 2007.

Steele, Ian K. *Warpaths: Invasions of North America*. New York: Oxford University Press, 1994.

Taylor, Alan. *American Colonies*. New York: Penguin, 2001.

Taylor, Alan. *Colonial America: A Very Short Introduction*. New York: Oxford University Press, 2012.

Townsend, Camilla. *Pocahontas and the Powhatan Dilemma*. New York: Hill & Wang, 2005.

Wallenstein, Peter. *Cradle of America: Four Centuries of Virginia History*. Lawrence: University Press of Kansas, 2007.

WEBSITES

Encyclopedia Virginia, http://encyclopediavirginia.org.
Guns, Germs, and Steel: PBS, http://www.pbs.org/gunsgerms steel/.

Library of Congress, Jamestown Primary Sources, http://www.loc.gov/teachers/classroommaterials/primarysourcesets/jamestown/.

The Pocahontas Archive, http://digital.lib.lehigh.edu/trial/pocahontas/index.php.

Virginia's First People: Past and Present, http://virginiaindians.pwnet.org/.

Virtual Jamestown, http://www.virtualjamestown.org/page2.html.

INDEX

Note: In this index, the following symbols are used: italicized numbers for maps or photos, *n* for footnotes, and *T* for the Timeline located before the main text.